Lifting the Mask

Who are you when no-one's looking?

by

Jo Naughton

Grosvenor House
Publishing Limited

Jo Naughton is hereby identified as author of this work in accordance with Section 77 of the Copyright, Designs and Patents Act 1988

This book is published by
Grosvenor House Publishing Ltd
28-30 High Street, Guildford, Surrey, GU1 3EL.
www.grosvenorhousepublishing.co.uk

A CIP record for this book
is available from the British Library

ISBN 978-1-908596-67-3

This book is dedicated to Paolo:
my love, my soul mate, my friend, my mentor.

Acknowledgements

Ken and Lois, thank you for bringing the healing love of God into my life

Larissa, thank you for your unswerving friendship through the good times and the bad

Tim, thank you for your editorial insights and hours of painstaking proofing

Harvest Church, thank you for all your love, encouragement and patience

Contents

Introduction

'Lifting the Mask' is a book of hope which, by God's grace, will bring you on a journey towards healing and wholeness. It reveals some secrets about the issues of the human heart, many of which are hidden in the chapters and verses of the Song of Songs.

The book is simple and practical and will help you realise the truth about yourself so that you can be free to enjoy life and fulfil your destiny.

Whether you endured a dysfunctional upbringing, bereavement, separation, disappointment, betrayal or rejection, life can hurt. By God's grace, this book will help heal, refresh and restore your soul.

If you have never read the Song of Songs in the middle of the Bible, I suggest you do. It's very short so it won't take you long. As you do, ask the Holy Spirit to introduce you to the two main characters – King Solomon and his wife, the Shulamite.

All names (and some details) have been changed to protect the identity of the people mentioned and Bible references are from the New King James unless otherwise stated.

God has a wonderful plan for your life. I believe that 'Lifting the Mask' will help you to uncover your place and unique purpose. It is no accident that you have this book in your hand - God is about to take you on a glorious journey of discovery and restoration.

Chapter 1

The Journey

I first met my husband in November 1994 at a fireworks party that I wasn't really invited to. We talked for some time that evening and I went home full of hope and excitement. Over the next fortnight we met up a few times, enjoying our new-found friendship. It was not long before he told me that he loved me and within a matter of weeks, we were engaged. Nothing had ever felt so natural and right. It seemed as though we'd always known each other and had always been together. To add to our happiness, God repeatedly confirmed that He was the One bringing us together. Less than a year after we met, we were married. My life started anew. Bliss!

But it wasn't. We were the best friends you could ever wish for. We would walk and talk and play and pray. We spent lots of time together and encouraged each other in the things of God. We both had great jobs, we had a lovely flat, a cute dog and were nurturing a small but growing ministry. But there was something wrong.

Day one of our marriage, as we awoke in a beautiful fifteenth century hotel in the middle of the English countryside, was the first time I rejected my husband. Until I was in his arms, I didn't realise that I couldn't always cope with intimacy. I remember we went for a walk that morning in the beautiful sunshine and wept.

I loved him dearly. I wasn't capable of loving anyone more than I loved him. But there was something about being very close that made me shut down. Everything inside me recoiled and closed up.

It was shortly after our tenth anniversary that I hit rock bottom. I couldn't bear the thought of continuing to refuse my husband's affections any more and I knew that he had had his fill of rejection. I was at risk of ruining the greatest relationship in my life and I decided that I had to do whatever it took to become the wife my husband needed and deserved.

Quite separately, I had been crying out to God to use me more in ministry. I was hungry for greater anointing in my life. I had no idea how related the two yearnings of my heart were. God took me on an incredible journey – it was painful but it was glorious.

Now when people meet me they are surprised to hear my stories of pain and dysfunction. I'm certainly not perfect but I'm a thousand times more healed than I was back then. I feel whole! I can be around people who are cleverer and stronger than me and be at peace with who I am. I can enjoy the company of people in authority without worrying about what they think of me (or my cheeky husband!) I can be misunderstood and openly mocked yet laugh along with the crowd at myself. It feels good to be secure.

Today, I have one of the best marriages I know. We still walk and talk, play and pray. We still spend time together and encourage each other and now we're even in full-time ministry together. But underneath all that, we also have the most wonderful relationship of love and affection. I'm not the perfect wife but I know my husband is happy.

It's not just my husband who has seen (and benefited) from the change. People in our church come up to me and say, "You used to seem very stand-offish but now I enjoy your company." Others commented that they used to think I was always too busy but now they knew I had time for them. I thought I was just focused but now I know that I was damaged. The more healed I became, the more fulfilled I felt and the more God was able to use me to minister to others.

I am still a work in progress. That doesn't make me feel incomplete, inadequate or discouraged. It reassures me that my wonderful Lord and Saviour will continue perfecting me by His Holy Spirit until I go to be with Him. I love being healed and I loved being changed to be more like Him.

I have enjoyed the fruits of my freedom so much that my desire now is to see everybody embrace their healing. Life hurts and there are very few people who escape unscathed. In fact, most of us need the healing love of the Lord to touch our lives in one way or another.

Just as the power of God can heal a sore throat and cancer, so the love of God can heal anyone from the disappointment of redundancy to the wreckage of decades of rape, abuse and abandonment. The Lord does not want us to live with any kind of heartache. At the cross He bore all our griefs and carried all our sorrows. However significant or small the damage to our hearts or lives may be, God is interested in healing us.

As I was praying about how I could share this amazing experience of restoration, the Holy Spirit opened up a wonderful revelation from His word to me which I have shared in this book.

By His grace, 'Lifting the Mask' will take you on a journey that ultimately leads to inner peace and contentment. It will be a different journey to mine. It will be your unique path to follow. You might find that each chapter is a step towards your goal of total restoration or there could be one or two chapters that are your keys to happiness. Whether you need every paragraph on every page or simply a reminder of the truth that sets you free, please open your heart to the Holy Spirit and allow the Lord to speak to you as you embark on this journey.

Prayer

Heavenly Father,

I thank you that you love me and have a wonderful plan for my life. I open up my heart to you once again and ask that you show me where I need your healing power in my life. I commit my heart and my soul into your hands.

Make me more like you.

In Jesus' name,

Amen.

Chapter 2

We've got issues!

"Do not look at me for I am dark, because the sun has burned me; my mother's children were angry with me" Song of Songs 1:6

The Song of Songs is a wonderful story about love - the love between a husband and a wife and between God and His bride, the Church. It reveals the intimate feelings between a man and a woman who were deeply in love. At times, you could be forgiven for blushing at the more blatant passages describing the young couple's passion and desire for each other. It certainly is about love. But hidden among the affection and romance are some profound secrets for healing hurting hearts.

You see, King Solomon's wife - the heroine of the Song of Songs - suffered when she was growing up. Her lasting memory of childhood was the bitter anger of her brothers who forced her to work for hours on end in the scorching sun. Her skin was so badly burned that it was permanently damaged. Even as a grown woman, she preferred to keep the telltale facial scars hidden from the glare of onlookers by wearing a veil. The Shulamite's experiences marked her identity to such an extent that she tells us about her upbringing right at the start of chapter one.

> ***"Do not look at me for I am dark, because the sun has burned me; my mother's sons were angry with me; they made me the keeper of the vineyards but my own vineyard I have not kept." Song of Songs 1:6***

Kings probably like to keep their problems private but for Solomon, who wrote the book, he could have put it like this: "Meet the wife, she's got issues!"

I can relate to this woman. Before God restored me, whenever I made new friends, it wouldn't be long before I gave them a glimpse of my imperfect world. I wouldn't say much - just enough to draw some sympathy and excuse any brassy behaviour. In the same vein, after tragedy hit our home, I would feel as though I hadn't really got to know someone until they knew about my heartbreak and had heard my story. I believe Solomon's sweetheart, the Shulamite, was like that. She wanted us to know that she had a history because it helped her to explain the way she was.

We don't know how old the Shulamite was or how long she had been with Solomon but we can see from scripture that she brought the issues of her upbringing into her adult life and marriage. Insecurity made her needy and demanding. Fear tormented her thoughts. However, we also discover how the healing love of the king brought her on a journey to restoration.

Many people have physical imperfections that they are embarrassed about: a protruding nose, buck teeth, bad acne and so on. Onlookers can be cruel and make extremely hurtful comments that scar people psychologically. The Shulamite was so ashamed of her appearance that she asked the world to look away and she wore a veil.

When your inner image is not healed, your outer image can add to the negative way you feel about yourself. Perhaps the Shulamite felt that her scars told a story of hatred and rejection. Whether the marks on her face were ugly to the eye or not, they were certainly a reminder to this young woman of the pain of her past.

This lady was surrounded by friends and married to the most eligible gentleman alive at the time. I don't think anyone could doubt the magnitude of her husband's devotion. A woman will often long for her boyfriend or husband to express unwavering affection in kind and passionate words of adoration. Solomon was the master of romantic poetry and exuberant affirmation. Yet we learn from the Bible that the troubles of her childhood still hampered our heroine's daily life.

What about you?

You might have made it to adult life without anyone noticing your buried pain. You may have an excellent education, an impressive job, a powerful ministry or a successful business. But if your heart isn't completely healed, you will never be able to live your life to the full. Your outer self might not be damaged like the Shulamite's was. Nonetheless, if you have never been restored after disappointment, rejection or trauma, you may never be able to fulfil your full potential.

Like Jacob in the Bible, you may be married to a wonderful woman, have a troupe of fantastic children and a brilliant career. However, again like Jacob, you may live under the shadow of unhealed memories. Jacob's issue was his relationship with his father, Isaac, who preferred his twin brother, Esau. You can have everything the world offers, but if you don't face the disappointments of bygone days, they may catch up with you and affect your future.

I had no idea that I was damaged. Of course, I knew that my family had known its share of pain and suffering, but I thought I had escaped relatively unscathed. I was alright. In fact, I thought I was thriving. It was only in the heat of marriage and the intensity of ministry that the past caught up with me.

On the other hand, you might be painfully aware of how the events of your past have affected your life, but perhaps you have never managed to find real freedom. I believe God has a plan to bring you out of your pain and into His good pleasure.

I have met countless people who have been crippled in adult life by childhood experiences. Debbie was abandoned by her mother when she was just ten. Left at home alone while her mum popped to the shops, she waited four long months for her to return. And although her mum came back, rejection had taken hold of this little girl. As an adult, that same rejection affected her relationships. She would seek to be affirmed by anyone who drew close, but her deep-seated hunger for love drove many away.

Eddie was abandoned by his father and raised by a volatile mother. To him, love always failed and trust was foolish. He couldn't relate well to men and would date older women who reminded him of his mother. He longed for security and yet pushed away those closest to him for fear of being rejected.

It was only when these precious people were brave enough to acknowledge their issues and allow God to heal them that they started to find real freedom and happiness in adult life.

I pray that this book will help lead you to greater wholeness and happiness. Many of the topics are based on the secrets hidden in the pages of Song of Songs and the chapters deal with one issue at a time. Whether you were wounded when you were growing up or have suffered in your adult life, I encourage you to open up your heart to the healing love of God. I suggest you find a quiet place where you won't be disturbed too much in order to read this and keep your heart open to the wonderful work of the Holy Spirit.

Chapter 3

Facing the truth

"Let me see your face." Song of Songs 2:14

The Shulamite woman wore a veil of lace to cover her pain. I used to wear a veil of success. I learned early on in life that doing well made me feel good. It gave me a sense of self-worth and value so I became a success-seeker. As long as I was achieving in education, in work, in family life, I felt important and feeling important made me feel good. My 'success' disguised the truth that I was full of insecurities and riddled with rejection. I didn't know that I needed healing. I thought I was fine.

Our heroine's face represented her pain. It was the evidence that her brothers had rejected and mistreated her. I believe that's one of the reasons why she covered it with a veil. In Song of Songs 1:6, this woman said what many of us think: "Do not look at me." She wanted to keep her painful past hidden but Solomon asked his wife to show him where she hurt: "Let me see your face." He asked her to expose the damage of her childhood so that he could love her back to health.

My story

Hurt people inevitably hurt people. I grew up in the north of England to wonderful parents. I never doubted their love. But my family experienced a great deal of trauma: mental illness, psychotic breakdown, violence, police involvement, court hearings, separation, a fire, loss of our possessions - the list could go on.

But I never considered myself to be wounded. The day I got my school results set my life on a particular course. I was 16 years of age and I did really well. The achievement gave me an enormous sense of self-worth and satisfaction. I was on a high. It felt like I'd taken a harmless drug and I liked the effects. I liked them very much. Unconsciously, I learned to seek success and that great feeling of adequacy and value it produced in me. When I succeeded, I felt I was significant. I had become a 'success junkie'.

My next exam results when I was 18 made for another good day, and my degree. When I was offered a job, again, it was a shot of my drug. Promotions, winning contracts, positions in church, recognition in Christian circles: they all gave me that same sense of self-worth. On all levels, I was doing relatively well. I gained early promotions to significant positions in major organisations. And at the same time, I was flourishing in my Christian life. Together with my husband, we were pastoring a small but growing church in London. I was very dedicated and loved God dearly. On the outside, I looked like a successful Christian woman (and I really believed I was). But on the inside, I was a mess. I found intimacy with my husband difficult. But of course, only he knew that. I was desperate for attention and affirmation, caring very much what others thought of me. And I was anxious around people in authority – like well-known pastors or highly successful friends or relatives.

On top of that, although I always had friends, a lot of people found me unapproachable or stand-offish. I thought that I was focused and task-oriented. In reality, I was prone to being abrupt and harsh.

But God heard my cry. It was not a cry for healing because I didn't know I needed this. My cry was a cry for God to use me to bring salvation and healing to the nations. The problem is that hurt people hurt people and God couldn't use me the way I was, so He had to heal me in order to use me. My prayer to be useful in the hands of God rose to His throne as a plea for healing. That, together with my desperate desire to have a genuinely happy marriage and family, led me on a new journey.

Your heart lies to you

> ***"The heart is deceitful above all things and desperately wicked; who can know it? I, the Lord, search the heart, I test the most secret parts."*** **Jeremiah 17:9-10**

This scripture tells us that one of the heart's greatest capabilities is deceit. Just as the heart is able to love and be loved, the heart is able to deceive and be deceived. Put simply, your heart can - and probably does - lie to you.

My heart told me I was fine. Philippians 3:13 says, "Forgetting what is behind." I took that powerful scripture but used it to blank out the past. I chose to forget. Forgetting is fine once you are healed (or for a season). Yet, unless you go on to be healed, it is counter-productive.

Rosie suffered terrible abuse at the hands of her uncle - the man who was supposed to be caring for her. She lived life for many decades avoiding the pain. She told herself that it was all behind her and that she was fine the way she was. In reality, she was bound by fear and shame and her hidden past affected many of her relationships. Then God shone the light of His truth into her heart and she stopped running away from those hideous memories.

Forty years after she was abused by her relative, this dear sister faced the shame she felt and acknowledged the pain buried deep inside. Soon she began a journey to genuine healing. It is never too soon or too late to allow God to heal you. He is always willing and always ready to bind up your wounds.

Not long after this precious lady opened her heart to God's healing love, the Lord started to give her a new ministry. Now He uses her to bring healing to the broken-hearted. She has a precious ministry and carries a marvellous anointing.

That's not the real me...

It's amazing how we manage to distance ourselves from our past. What do I mean? I would like you to picture yourself at your most vulnerable period - the time in your life of greatest rejection or abuse, the chapter in your story when you were jilted, bullied or abandoned. Picture that child, young person or adult right now. What do you see? Who do you see?

Do you see a little boy or a little girl that you warm towards, that you love? Do you see yourself at your prime of life? Or, like many others, do you see an awkward, perhaps unlikeable child or older person?

All too often, because we dislike the memory of suffering, we end up disliking the person who suffered and distance ourselves from them. It's a way of disassociating ourselves from the pain and resulting shame. We think to ourselves, "That person makes me cringe. That's not the real me. That's not who I am anymore."

If you see someone you don't really like, I encourage you to ask God to heal your self-image. When others reject us, we all too easily reject ourselves. I remember that I used to have an unpleasant picture of myself as a child. I saw a loud, irritating show-off. Most of my memories were of a little girl I didn't like, but as God healed me, He changed my heart.

I remember reading a book by John and Paula Sanford that helped me enormously. I read their book on a long-haul flight and had plenty of time to absorb its teachings. I remember sitting in my window seat and picturing myself as a seven year old. At first, I recoiled from the child I saw in my mind's eye, but then I approached her and told her that she was fearfully and wonderfully made. I told her that God loved her and had a wonderful plan for her life. I gave her a big hug and told her that I accepted her just the way she was. It was a remarkably healing experience and it changed my view of myself. Now I know I was a lovely little girl. Why don't you do what I did and open your heart to the person you once were? Love that child of God that He has always loved and accept them just as He does.

Why am I like that?

I have learned much from how Rebekah, Isaac's wife, handled her first pregnancy. After twenty years of believing God for a child, Rebekah finally became pregnant. But after all those years of hoping and waiting, when she finally conceived, it didn't feel right. She wasn't reacting the way she expected. Perhaps she was in pain or intensely uncomfortable. So Rebekah asked herself, "If all is well, then why am I like this? And she went to inquire of the Lord." (Genesis 25:22) God answered Rebekah and told her why things felt strange. She was pregnant with twins.

Are you embarrassed or defensive when people make fun of you or point out your mistakes? Are you shy, always avoiding the spotlight? Maybe you are aggressive, abrupt or very task-oriented? Perhaps you're highly competitive and can't bear it when you are beaten or lose? Are you in constant need of affirmation and reassurance? Are you too easily put down by the reactions, facial expressions or comments of others?

It's all too easy to say, "That's my personality, that's just the way I am. I was made this way and you have to take the rough with the smooth."

But you weren't made that way. I have never met a shy or abrupt baby! The Bible tells us that we were made in the image of God and I don't see any of these characteristics in Jesus – our role model and our standard. Something in your distant and recent past caused you to become like that. Most of us could learn from Rebekah. When you ask God why you are the way you are, when you ask Him to show you what makes you react the way you do, He shines His light in your heart and exposes the issues deep within.

In the first few years of pastoring with my husband, two or three people made comments to me about my attitude and behaviour. After one lady got to know me, she revealed that she had previously found me really unapproachable. Another woman said she watched a church member give me a hug and was amazed at her boldness! She didn't think anyone would be able to do this. I was taken aback by these comments and more than a little upset.

I talked with a few close friends. One told me that I was a powerful woman of God who was just very focused and I should not be distracted by their comments. It was tempting to believe that dear sister. But in my heart, I knew that if something about me pushed people away then something was wrong. Jesus is never aloof or detached. He is always there to love and encourage. I had to inquire, "If all is well, Lord, then why am I like this?"

If you ask God to show you what is hidden in your heart, He will reveal it to you. Since that first occasion, I have learned to go to God time and time again. For example, if I have over-reacted in a situation, I go to the Lord and say, "If all is well, then why did I react like that?" If I have become disproportionately anxious, again I ask the Lord why. God invariably exposes the issues of my heart to me. Often it's an unhealed memory or perhaps a hidden resentment.

King David regularly asked God to expose the issues of his heart to him. He wanted to be whole and he wanted to be used by God.

> ***"Search me thoroughly O God and know my heart. Try me and know my thoughts. And see if there is any wicked (twisted) or hurtful way in me and lead me in the way everlasting." (Psalm 139 23-24 Amplified Version)***

Verse twenty three in The Message Bible opens up the passage further: "Investigate my life, O God, find out everything about me; cross-examine and test me, get a clear picture of what I'm about." God knows what is really going on in the secret caverns of our souls and He is able to reveal the truth to us.

> ***"You alone know the hearts of the sons of men." 2 Chronicles 6:30***

David's prayer in Psalm 139 might seem like a difficult prayer to pray or step to take but it will start you on the journey to eventual healing. It will lead you in the way everlasting.

You need the truth

God is the God of truth. The Holy Spirit is called the Spirit of Truth. He desires truth from us: truth in our innermost being, truth in the secret places of our hearts. God desires to reveal the secrets that are bound up in our hearts – things that we may not even know.

> ***"You desire truth in the inward parts." Psalm 51:6***

Truth is so important to God that when Jesus was dedicated to God as a baby, Mary received a prophecy that there was a mandate on her Son's life to expose people's thinking.

> ***"A sword will pierce through your own soul... that the thoughts of many hearts may be revealed." Luke 2:35***

Why does the Lord want us to face the truth? That's simple. He loves us and it's the truth that will set us free from the pain, shame, regret and sadness of the past.

> ***"You shall know the truth and the truth shall set you free." John 8:32***

However, sometimes the truth is hard to hear. One day, my husband and I were having lunch in a hotel restaurant with my spiritual parents, Pastors Ken and Lois Gott. Unbeknown to me, Lois, who had known me since my teenage years, had been praying that God would heal my wounded heart. As we ate, she asked me a question: "Do you think you were rejected when you were growing up?" I sat and thought. I had always known that my parents loved me so I responded, "No."

I sat in silence for a few moments reflecting on my life. Lois asked me the question again. This time I broke down and wept. I cried for nearly half an hour. That was the beginning of my journey of healing. It began when I faced the truth that I didn't feel wanted. I didn't feel good enough.

Jacob's journey

> ***"Esau was a cunning hunter, a man of the field; Jacob was a plain man, dwelling in tents. And Isaac (their father) loved Esau." Genesis 25:27-28***

I have learned so much about the ways of God from Jacob's life. Let's look at his story. Jacob grew up knowing that his father preferred his brother, Esau. Esau was strong. He was an outdoor man – his father's type. By contrast, Jacob was his mother's favourite, but that wasn't enough. Rejection took hold in his heart.

From his youth, Jacob went about things the wrong way. He competed with the people around him, cheated to get what he wanted and lied to those he loved. Ultimately, Jacob made an enemy of his own brother.

I doubt very much whether this young man ever felt the assurance of his father's approval. He probably never heard the words, "I love you just because you're my son."

Jacob knew that God had a great plan for his life, but I believe that insecurity motivated him as much as destiny. Subconsciously, he probably wanted to demonstrate that he was good enough; that his father was wrong to reject him and favour Esau.

For years, Jacob tried to make a success of things. He had a good relationship with God, a loving wife, children and a very prosperous business. But he was still striving for acceptance.

It wasn't until Jacob faced the truth that his life really changed. If you are reading this book, hopefully you are asking God to do a work in you. Jacob reached the point when he wanted God to completely change his nature. But this could only happen when he faced the truth. In Genesis 32:27, Jacob had an encounter with God. And God asked him, "What is your name?" This might seem an odd question for God to ask. God knows everything, so why did He ask Jacob his name?

At Jacob's birth, Isaac demonstrated his immediate disdain for this son by calling him 'deceiver' or 'fraudster.' That's what the name Jacob means. And Jacob fulfilled his father's low expectations, cheating his way through life. When God asked Jacob his name, He was asking him to acknowledge the reason he was given his name. He was asking Jacob to face his hurts and to accept his issues. He was asking Jacob to recognise the bad decisions he had made throughout his life and the very wrong way he had gone about things.

When Jacob faced the truth about himself, he reached the greatest turning point of his life. God met Him at his point of turmoil and gave him a new identity. Instead of deceiver or fraudster, God called him Israel, which means 'prince with God.' His earthly father branded him a liar, but his heavenly father restored him and gave him a new identity as a royal partner of the Most High. Through this man, the Lord raised up an entire nation which carried Jacob's new name. Through this man, God established twelve tribes that would lead God's chosen people. But without truth, there could have been no exchange.

If God were to ask you the same question, how would you respond? What is the overwhelming issue that has dogged your life and marked your identity? Is your name failure, or rejected, or intimidated, or unpopular, or loner, or detached, or insecure, or people-pleaser? What is your name?

Lifting the mask

King Solomon asked the Shulamite to lift her mask – a veil – and show him the scars of her suffering. In the same way, God is asking you and I to remove our masks. For some of you, the mask may represent denial. You say your upbringing didn't affect you and you have just moved on. You don't have much contact with the people who have hurt you (if they are still alive) or you maintain 'professional' relationships with others. You are possibly not very good at genuine intimacy or at sharing truth. The problem is that pain festers and infects. Ultimately it can break us:

> ***"A merry heart makes a cheerful countenance but by sorrow of the heart the spirit is broken." Proverbs 15:13***

For others it might be a mask of avoidance. You steer clear of even thinking about the things you experienced. I have met many people who have never talked about the abuse they suffered in their childhood. It's too painful and just thinking about it brings shame.

For another group, the mask is substitution. Rather than denying that the past affected you or avoiding the pain, you try to fill the void of love and acceptance with other things. Perhaps you are a workaholic. Perhaps you crave success or recognition. You may have a driven personality. There is a vast range of emotional 'drugs' we use to try and fill the void. But every high that comes from success or a commendation from your boss will only be temporary. Once the high wears off, you will be seeking your next fix.

God is asking us to lift the mask, to show Him how we have been damaged by the people around us. God loves you very much. He loves you completely. He is not repelled by the ugliness that repels you. He loves you. The first step in dealing with pain is to face it. You need to face the truth.

> ***"When the Spirit of truth comes, He will take you by the hand and guide you into all the truth." John 16:13 (New Living Translation)***

Invite the Spirit of Truth into your heart right now. Ask Him to come and take you by the hand and lead you into all the truth. Make a choice today to refuse any deceit in your heart. Although the truth hurts, it brings freedom.

Prayer

Heavenly Father,

Thank you that you know me completely. You know the deep issues of my heart and the experiences of my life that have made me the way I am.

I acknowledge my issues (tell God your issues – are you defensive, competitive, a people-pleaser, afraid of confrontation, anxious around certain people, shy, self-conscious?)

I ask you to show me why I am the way I am. If all is well, then why am I like this? Open my eyes to see what you see. Only you know the truth and I ask you to show it to me.

From now on, I am committed to the truth. Where I have denied the truth because it was too unpleasant or avoided the truth because it was too painful, please forgive me. You desire truth in the inward parts and from now on, I desire truth too.

Holy Spirit of Truth, please come and take me by the hand and lead me into all the truth from this day forth - one step at a time and one day at a time. Thank you that as I face the truth, you will heal me and set me free to become the person you designed me to be.

It is in Jesus' name that I pray,

Amen

Chapter 4

The marks of rejection

"I opened for my beloved, but my beloved had turned away and was gone."
Song of Songs 5:6

One evening, the Shulamite had a very upsetting dream. This is what happened. The King, her husband, came to the door in the middle of the night to see her, but because she was already undressed and in bed, she was slow in responding to his knocking. By the time she arose, he was gone. He probably reckoned: "She must be sound asleep. I don't want to disturb my darling love."

But that's not what the Shulamite thought. You can almost hear the fear in her words, "But my beloved had turned away and was gone." She continued, probably with a knot in her stomach: "I sought him but I could not find him; I called him, but he gave me no answer." (Song of Songs 5:6b)

When you have been marked by rejection, normal events can deepen your sense of fear and insecurity. In the dream, the Shulamite's husband had just left. Not forever, not because he didn't love her and not because she had done something to upset him. It was just because she didn't answer the door in the night. When you are wounded, you can end up reading rejection into nearly every action of others.

You call someone and they don't phone back. Rejection. You see someone dear to you and they look away. Rejection. You go to talk to your pastor and he walks away. Rejection. You seek a new job or a promotion and you are turned down. Rejection. The truth is that until your heart is healed, you are going to see the events of your life through a damaged lens.

It is impossible for a wounded person to keep their hurts out of their closest relationships. This can often be the root of dysfunction in marriage. The Shulamite probably wanted to be the perfect wife, especially as she was married to the most eligible man in the land! However, because of her unhealed heart, she brought rejection and insecurity into the marriage. Whatever stage you are at in life, you can be healed - whether you are young or old, at the top of your tree or out of work, single or married. You *can* be restored.

The evidence of your healing will be seen and felt by many - especially by those closest to you. You'll have new security and assurance, quiet confidence and real contentment However, until you allow the healing love of God to restore your heart, your pain will spill out into your most important relationships.

The Shulamite completely overreacted to the circumstances. But this was not the first time she had exposed her insecurities and allowed her fear of rejection to control her behaviour.

"By night on my bed, I sought the one I love; I sought him but I did not find him. "I will rise now," I said, "And go about the city; in the streets and in the squares I will seek the one I love." Song of Songs 3:1-2

Imagine the scene (this is not a dream). The Shulamite wakes up and finds that her husband isn't home yet. Remember that she is married to a very busy man – the ruler of Israel! Instead of rolling over in bed and praying for him, she panics. At a time in history when women were expected to be in the home, she gets up in the middle of the night and starts running around the city, crying out for Solomon. She probably put herself in danger. She might have embarrassed the king and she certainly exposed her vulnerabilities. Rejection makes you react inappropriately. It fills you with insecurity and fear and leads you to read all sorts of things into the normal behaviour of others.

Rejection is probably one of the most painful and harmful human emotions. Even Jesus recognised that one of the hardest things He would have to endure was rejection:

"He must suffer many things <u>and be rejected</u> by this generation." Luke 17:25

He also acknowledged the added pain of being rejected by people in positions of authority, whether parents, pastors, employers, leaders or teachers. Jesus put the pain of rejection up there with the pain of death:

"The Son of Man must suffer many things and be rejected by the elders and chief priests and scribes, and be killed..." Luke 9:22

If you have suffered rejection, it will be really important to allow God into the inner caverns of your soul. As I said in chapter three, the starting point is truth. You need to acknowledge that you were rejected. Or at least, that you felt rejected. Perhaps you were rejected by your father or mother. Maybe nothing you did was good enough when you were growing up and even now you feel inadequate. When parents constantly drive their children to achieve and perform, youngsters often believe they're saying, "You're not good enough the way you are." It can end up planting a root of rejection in even the strongest of little souls.

Favouritism in the family can cause deep wounds in the heart of a vulnerable child. Jacob knew that his dad, Isaac, loved his brother, Esau, best. As a result, I believe Jacob spent much of his life striving to prove his value. Maybe you felt like the black sheep of the family or the runt of the litter. It can mark your life forever.

Then there are the serious wounds of sexual abuse. This is perhaps one of the most difficult and confusing forms of rejection. With one hand you are shunned and with the other you are pulled close and violated. Your childhood and innocence are stolen from you and you are sworn to an isolating secrecy.

Physical abuse goes deeper than the blows to the skin, however serious the bodily harm. The emotional damage will almost always be more severe.

Maybe you were rejected in love or marriage. I always say that pain in love is some of the deepest we can ever feel. Even in a great relationship, being misunderstood or spurned can be excruciating. Add unfaithfulness, betrayal, violence or disinterest to the mix and the effects can be devastating.

Discrimination because of your skin colour, background or accent is another huge area of damage.

Whatever caused the wounding, it is vital that you face and accept the truth - that you felt rejected and you didn't feel you were good enough.

King David knew of the agony of being alienated by those closest to him and expressed his disbelief and disappointment to the Lord in prayer:

> ***"My loved ones and my friends stand aloof..." Psalm 38:11***

He understood the grief of betrayal by those he trusted and he poured out his sorrow before God:

> ***"It was you, a man my equal, my companion and my acquaintance." (who betrayed me) Psalm 55:13-14***

From the place of truth we can start to receive the healing power of God. Fact must always submit to truth and, although you may have been rejected by man (fact), you have been chosen and accepted by God (truth).

As you read on, you will learn about the importance of releasing trapped words. The human soul is often like a bottle with a cork in the top, trapping all the emotions and pain inside. Rejection can be harboured deep within the soul but words are the route to letting the pain out so that you can start to allow God's healing love in.

Prayer

Dear Lord,

This is really hard. Nevertheless, I come to you today and acknowledge that I was rejected. I haven't really thought of it like that before but now I see that the things that have happened to me have made me feel as though I wasn't good enough and that I wasn't wanted.

I felt rejected by (name the person or people that you feel rejected you) and it left me broken.

I come to you today and I ask you to start the process of healing my heart. I realise that I have reacted to the people around me through my pain. I have seen the actions of others through the lens of my own rejection and I don't want to carry on like that anymore.

Come Holy Spirit and bring your healing power into my heart.

In Jesus' name I pray,

Amen

Chapter 5

Sticks and stones may break my bones

"You are all fair, my love; there is no spot in you." Song of Songs 4:7

Psychologists say that a normal healthy person needs four positive words to counteract every negative word spoken over their life. Perhaps you grew up surrounded by words of disappointment, or comparison with brothers, sisters or friends. Maybe you heard people who were supposed to love you tell you that you weren't good enough or clever enough. If so, those comments will probably have left a festering scar in your soul.

King Solomon knew that the Shulamite needed to hear words of love and acceptance. In fact, in just seven chapters, he told her twelve times that she was fair. He declared that she was "the fairest among women." Her view of herself was that she was dark and she chose to cover herself. We see the tell-tale signs of both self-hatred and shame in her heart. But the King challenged her self-image by speaking over her again and again and again to say that, in his eyes, she was beautiful.

Framed and formed by words

The Bible says in Hebrews 11:3 that "God (our Father) framed the world by His words". In the same way, our world is framed when we are growing up by the words of our parents. Just as a young plant climbs up a frame or a trellis, so a child is nurtured and formed by their father and mother's words. It's not only negative words which damage a youngster. The absence of positive words creates a horrible vacuum. Without the right affirmation and encouragement, a child can lack security and stability.

Perhaps you never knew your dad. Or if you did, maybe he hardly gave you any attention. When he did notice you, it was in the form of harsh and critical words or a heartless beating. Maybe your mother had so many problems of her own that she couldn't love you the way you needed to be loved. I know the kind of marks that such circumstances can leave on a young life.

Children need affirmation to become secure, confident adults. If you were deprived of assurance and approval when you were growing up, it has probably affected your whole life.

If you have never known the unconditional approval of a loving parent, or if you have never been clothed in words of affirmation, it will be really important to ask your heavenly Father to come into this area of your life.

In James 3, the Bible likens the tongue to a ship's rudder. Words which you speak about yourself direct the course of your life. However, so do the words that others speak about you if you believe them and don't counteract them if they are negative. The problem is that when we're children, most of us believe everything we are told. Santa Claus and the Tooth Fairy are evidence of this. So why wouldn't we believe every word spoken to us by those who are older and supposedly wiser?

Teachers hold a position of great responsibility in children's lives because their words carry authority. There are two minor episodes from my school days that stuck in my mind for years after they occurred. Strangely enough, I can't really remember any of my teachers' names, except those of the two involved in these accounts.

Mr Hewitt used to give everyone nicknames. Some were more flattering than others but those he gave to me made me feel ashamed. He would alternate between calling me 'rubber lips' and 'funny face'. I don't think I was very self-conscious before that time, but I started to feel awkward about myself when I was in his class. I thought I was someone that other people put up with rather than a girl whom others wanted to have around. His words influenced my negative view of myself.

In secondary school, I had a very strict science tutor, Miss Green. She would have sudden outbursts of anger that terrified me so I always tried my hardest when I was in her class. Admittedly, I was a terrible attention-seeker so I probably irritated my teachers no end, but all I really wanted was a few words of encouragement.

One day my hand shot up when Miss Green asked a question. As she turned to me, my mind went completely blank. In an attempt to allay her response, I hesitated and said, "I'm trying my hardest." She was furious and hurled the blackboard rubber across the classroom at me as she retorted, "Yes, Joanne, you are always very trying!" I felt squashed by her comment. My friends sniggered and my self-image was dented again.

Not much changes as we grow older. People tend to find it easier to believe the worst. Even as adults, we are all too often wounded by the words of those we love or admire. And those wounds will be deeper if we have not been healed of childhood hurts.

There is a popular school saying that goes, "Sticks and stones may break my bones, but words will never hurt me." Although I recognise the value of encouraging children not to take the unkind words of others to heart, this is a lie. The Bible sets the record straight:

> ***"Death and life are in the power of the tongue..." Proverbs 18:21***

I have met many people who have been crippled by words. I believe God mentioned death before life in this verse because people use words to hurt, wound and destroy more often than they do to speak life. Sadly, negative comments are usually a lot easier to believe than positive ones.

> ***"There is one who speaks like the piercings of a sword, but the tongue of the wise promotes health." Proverbs 12:18***

Just as a sword can pierce the heart of a man and kill his body, so a hurtful word can penetrate a delicate soul and leave a festering wound.

Alan was a quietly confident young man who ended up with an aggressive and dysfunctional boss. Mildly negative comments soon turned into blatant bullying and, day in day out, Alan had to come to work to face a team who ridiculed him and dismissed any contributions he made. Nothing was 'off limits' so he was mocked for his dress sense as well as his creative ideas.

In truth, his manager probably felt threatened by his quick thinking and general intelligence. Within a matter of months, Alan had gone from being a relatively secure young man with great promise to a bag of nerves. Words had demolished his self-confidence and he was left feeling terribly inadequate. It was only after he worked for a believer who invested a great deal of time and energy in building him back up that his true potential shone once again. After a year going backwards, he started to make real progress.

If you have been marked by hurtful words, you need to be healed. To receive restoration, we need to remove the painful words from our heart as though we were removing thorns from our flesh – one by one. We need to tell the Lord what was said and how it made us feel. We then need to replace those painful piercings with words of love.

Stamp of approval

Before Jesus lifted a finger in ministry, God told the world in Matthew 3:6, "This is my beloved Son in whom I am well pleased." Jesus knew that His Father loved Him. He knew that His Father approved of Him. His identity had been positively marked by His affirmation. Jesus was perfectly secure.

Out of this security, He could fulfil God's plan for His life. Out of this security, He could do the right thing even when the crowds and leaders hated Him. Out of this security, He went to the cross. He was totally secure in His Father's love.

> ***"As many as received Him, to them He gave the right to become children of God." John 1:12***

When we accept Jesus as our Lord, we become children of God. And when you are a son or a daughter of God, He loves you just the way He loves Jesus. He loves you because you are His child, not because you do good things. In fact, He loves you even when you don't do good things. He loves you just because you are His.

Jesus told a story in Luke 15 about two brothers. One lived the high life, partying, sleeping around and squandering his dad's hard-earned money. The other stayed at home and always did the right thing. The father loved them both. They were his sons.

When the partygoer hit rock bottom and came back, the father opened his heart and home to him again. Luke 15:20 says: "But when the son was still a great way off, the father saw him and had compassion and ran to meet him and hugged him and kissed him."

Whatever you have or haven't done, your Father in heaven loves you and accepts you because you are His. God's heart towards you is the same as His heart towards

Jesus. He says to you, "You are my beloved child and in you I am well pleased."

Shut your eyes right now and receive these words to your heart from your Father in heaven. You are His dearly treasured and beloved child and He is really pleased with you. That is not dependent on what you do but on who you are and who you belong to. You are His and He is delighted.

Allow those words to touch your heart. You may need to write them on a card and put them on your wall until you believe them. King Solomon told the Shulamite again and again that he loved her. He challenged her self-image. She said: "I am dark", but he said, "You are all fair." Don't think that you know yourself better than anyone else. You don't. God does:

> ***"Oh Lord you have searched me thoroughly and You know me." Psalm 139:1 (Amplified)***

He knows everything about you and in the light of everything He knows, He loves you completely. You may say, "I am a failure" or "I am unlovable" or "No-one really wants me" but your Dad in heaven says, "I'm pleased with you. I love you just the way you are and I want you to be with Me always."

It's important that you deal with the words spoken to you and about you and face what you really think about yourself. Ask the Holy Spirit to expose your innermost thoughts to you. Then you need to allow the truth of God's Word and His love to fill your heart with a new perspective.

Prayer

Father in heaven,

Thank You that You believe in me. You know me inside out and You still love me. I bring the hurtful words to You that have been said to me and about me. (Be specific and tell the Lord who said what, how it made you feel and how it affected your self-image)

I break the power of every negative word over my life and I declare that no weapon formed against me will prosper. By faith, I remove every fiery dart that pierced my soul and I ask You to heal the wounds they created.

I choose to believe that You, Lord, take great delight in me. I thank You that You know me and love me. I am Yours and You are mine. I thank You that I am Your beloved child and that You are well pleased with me.

In Jesus' name, I pray,

Amen

Chapter 6

Unblocking the soul

"Let me hear your voice for your voice is sweet..." Song of Songs 2:14b

King Solomon knew that if he was going to help the love of his life to be healed, he would have to encourage her to talk. But it wasn't out of necessity that he drew her to speak. The king loved to hear his wife's voice because her words meant the world to him.

Someone wants to hear what you've got to say

If you have experienced rejection or abuse during your life, you might not believe that anyone is really interested in what you have to say. Perhaps the lack of love in your childhood has made you an out-and-out attention seeker – doing whatever it takes to get some sort of reaction. You think you have to put on a performance to get your share of the limelight. Who would want to sit down and just listen?

Alternatively, your life experiences may have caused you to shut down. You don't tell anyone anything meaningful. No one knows the real you, and your hopes and fears. Opening up sounds frightening. And anyway, who would want to listen for as long as it takes?

The things we go through can lower the value we place on our own views and opinions. If we have been put down, rejected or overlooked in the past, we can end up believing that it was because we are of little worth to others and what we think and say are unimportant. But that is a lie. You have a Lord and Saviour who loves to hear you share from your heart. He treasures you and every word you say.

If we want to be healed, we need to learn to speak out and release the words and thoughts that have been trapped inside us for years or even decades. The words we thought but never said, the things we wanted to tell but never could. To do that, we must believe that someone wants to hear them.

I remember my first date with the man who would become my husband. We went for a coffee near the church that we both attended and we talked for about three hours. What touched me most was not his wit, intelligence or even his spiritual hunger. It was his genuine interest in me. He asked me about myself and paid close attention to everything I said. I felt completely comfortable and accepted by him. I was able to relax and open up.

I remember feeling like a clockwork mouse, tightly wound up. But as I sat in his presence, I began to unwind and relax. That's the way the Lord listens to you, with genuine interest, loving-kindness and acceptance.

I want you to know that what you feel *is* important. What you suffered *does* matter. What you think *is* precious. Your King loves to hear you talk. He loves to hear the sound of your voice. He loves it when you open your heart to Him and pour out your innermost thoughts. King Solomon's love for the Shulamite is a picture of God's love for you: He loves to hear your voice, He wants to hear your voice and to Him your voice is sweet.

> ***"The companions listen for your voice – let me hear it!" Song of Songs 8:13***

Letting go

Hannah, who was soon to be the mother of Samuel the prophet, understood the importance of telling God everything. She was very disappointed with her life. I have already talked about the importance of truth. If you feel that your life so far has been one big disappointment then it's time to be honest because truth brings freedom.

Hannah's greatest desire and lifelong dream was to be a mum. Her husband loved her very much but that wasn't enough. She desperately wanted a baby. Sometimes we can be afraid of being honest about how we feel in case we sound ungrateful for what we have received. Hannah reached rock bottom. She went to the temple and released all her anger, pain and sadness before the Lord. She cried out in anguish and told God exactly how she felt. She didn't conceal her disappointment or hold back her bitterness. She spoke about it ALL to God. She was so loud and so vocal in her outpourings that Eli thought she was drunk. She put him straight and revealed that she had been pouring out her agony in prayer:

> ***"I am a woman of sorrowful spirit. I have drunk neither wine nor intoxicating drink, but have poured out my soul before the Lord... out of the abundance of my complaint and grief I have spoken until now." I Samuel 1:15-16***

It was when Hannah let go and released every thought and word before the Lord that her life started to change. It was when she was honest and real that God heard from heaven. Not long after her outpouring, Hannah became pregnant and gave birth to a baby boy who grew up to be probably the greatest prophet that the world had yet seen.

Say it like it is, not how you think He wants to hear it

When my eight year old daughter has had a difficult day at school, I know about it as soon as I see her. She comes running across the playground and straight into my arms. She immediately starts to tell me what has happened. "Elizabeth and Mary wouldn't let me play. They said I would spoil their game," she will explain. "And then Rachel walked off so I had to sit all by myself at break!"

By this time she will be in floods of tears and getting a reassuring cuddle. Within a matter of minutes, her tears will have dried up and she will be feeling much better. We have a great deal to learn from children.

> ***"Then Jesus called a little child to Him, set him in the midst of them, and said, 'Assuredly I say to you, unless you are converted (change your nature) and become as little children, you will by no means enter the kingdom of heaven."' (Matthew 18:3; parentheses mine)***

Picture this scene. Jesus was teaching His disciples how they should relate to one another and to God. He took a little boy by the hand and asked him to stand in the middle of the group of strong, burly men. Jesus told them that they needed to think, trust and talk like children. The example was a young boy, perhaps the same age as my daughter.

In Matthew 12:34, Jesus also said, "Out of the abundance of the heart the mouth speaks." God's plan is that the issues of our heart come out. We were made by our Creator God that way. Our bodies are like that too. If we hold urine in, it can cause infection. If we hold faeces in, it can cause constipation. In the same way, if we hold trapped words and memories in the secret caverns of our soul, it can damage our emotions and bind us up on the inside.

> ***"The kingdom of God is not eating and drinking but righteousness and peace and joy in the Holy Spirit." Romans 14:17***

There is a depth of peace and genuine joy available to us in this life, where we are at ease with ourselves: confident and comfortable. There is a place where we can live free from insecurity, rejection and painful emotions. But to enter that life, we must release the pain of the past and one of the most important ways in which that pain is released is through words.

> ***"Open up for me my sister, my love, my dove, my perfect one." Song of Songs 5:2b***

In this verse, King Solomon is telling the Shulamite what kind of words he wants to hear.

I am very talkative but I only learned to open up about the deep issues of my heart in the last six or seven years. When God was healing me, I used to set aside some time at the end of every week to be in His presence. During the week, I would ask the Lord to bring to mind the memories and wounds that He wanted to heal. Then every Friday morning, on my day off, I would open my heart to Him.

I would tell Him about the memories and hurts that He had brought to the fore that week. I would explain exactly what had happened, just like a child, and I would tell Him how those experiences made me feel. For two or three months, I set aside time every week to talk to God about my life and I knew He was listening. I would open up and God would heal. It was a life-changing season.

Be real

King David knew how to be real with the Lord. He knew that as he told God the truth, it would enable him to keep his heart clean and whole. He would spend hours in the presence of the Lord, recounting his fears, worries and struggles.

> ***"I pour out my complaint before Him, I declare before Him my trouble." Ps 142:2***

Read any of David's Psalms and you will see him doing just that. David was a strong, successful leader and yet he knew how to release his pain before his Saviour. He would lament the injustices he saw around him. "Why do I suffer even though I serve you while evildoers seem to escape?" He would be completely honest about his grievances yet always end up praising God in spite of his anguish.

> ***"Pour out your heart before the Lord. He is a refuge." Psalm 62:8***

He didn't try to distance himself from his difficulties. Instead, he acknowledged his struggles and laid everything at the feet of the Lord, knowing that God was not in the least bit shocked. God doesn't get worried when we tell the truth. No, He is relieved that at last we are opening up to Him in the knowledge that He is able to set us free.

For God to deal with a problem, we have to give it to Him. When we talk, that's exactly what we are doing. We make our problems His problems and He is far more able to solve them than we are! David knew that God was his safe 'refuge', the place where he could be himself without fear of rejection or judgment, and the place where he would be healed and strengthened. David was a man of faith, but it didn't stop Him telling the Lord when he felt weak. He would exchange his weakness for God's strength and his troubles for God's help.

> ***"Have mercy on me, O Lord, for I am weak; O Lord heal me, for my bones are troubled. My soul also is greatly troubled ... I am weary with my groaning." Psalm 6:2-3, 6***

This is agony!

The book of Lamentations gives us another example of a mighty man laying the questions of his heart before the Lord. Jeremiah was a national prophet, a strong man and a great leader who was not afraid of confrontation at the highest level. This same Jeremiah told God about his pain and shame, asked questions and released the words of turmoil trapped in his soul.

> ***"See, O Lord, that I am in distress; my soul is troubled; my heart is overturned within me." Lamentations 1:20***

> ***"I have become the ridicule of all my people – their taunting song all the day." Lamentations 3:14***

Releasing hurts before God is not a sign of weakness. It is probably a sign of great strength. This spiritual giant who knew the heart of God and of man not only brought his own issues to God. He also exhorted the people to come before God with their concerns:

> ***"Pour out your heart like water before the face of the Lord." Lamentations 2:19***

So how do we get started?

As adults, we can analyse our lives and talk about events of the past in a rather detached way. That's not what children do. We need to change our nature and become like them. We need to revert to the way we were made. It's one thing to say, "My father left when I was six. It was a difficult time for everybody, but we made it through in the end." It's something else to release the words which were trapped in when you were six and the feelings you felt but never shared. "Why did you leave? What did I do wrong? You abandoned me and left me at home with mum. I had to grow up without you there. I always felt embarrassed at school when they talked about families. I felt so angry and so sorry and so hurt..."

The first approach keeps you a safe distance from your pain and ensures you don't feel too much. The latter is more difficult, but it will help you release the angst that has been buried inside you, bound up in trapped words.

I would like to suggest that you do what I did: find a regular time for just you and Jesus. Commit to being open with God and pour out your heart before Him during those occasions. Ask the Lord to bring back the memories and events of the past that He wants to heal. He will work at the right pace for you, never too fast or too slow.

He knows you completely and He wants to heal you entirely. It might be one memory a week or it might be more. And it might be a month or a lot longer. Don't tell Him about the event. Imagine that you are back there. Tell Him what happened and how it made you feel. As you talk and open up, ask Him to heal your heart. It won't take long before you start to feel the burden lifting and the pain easing. Although you may be particularly vulnerable for a season, know that God is at work to bring you through.

> ***"Let us hold fast the confession of our hope without wavering, for He who promised is faithful." Hebrews 10:23***

Prayer

Lord God,

I want to start being real with You. Please help me to come to You as a dearly loved child would approach their father. Enable me to open up my heart and tell You about my life. I believe that You want to hear what I have to say and I know that as I share with You, You will heal me. Help me to remember that You care about what I have gone through because You care about me.

(Now I encourage you to start to talk to God about something that happened to you. Narrate the experience, tell Him how you felt and ask the questions buried inside. As you talk, know that you have the Lord's complete attention. Then ask Him to heal you of those experiences. You may have to revisit certain memories more than once. You'll know when you're free.)

In Jesus' name I pray,

Amen

Chapter 7

Don't make me cry

"Weeping may endure for the night but joy comes in the morning." Psalm 30:5

In 2000, five years after my husband and I were married, our two year old daughter suddenly died. We were devastated. She was a beautiful little girl with bright blue eyes, blonde curly hair and a magnetic personality. Naomi was a cheeky, happy, healthy toddler without a care in the world. But on a sunny day that April, she was snatched from us. A bacterial infection caused multiple organ failure and, thirty hours after being admitted to hospital, she was gone. Just like that.

After the shock subsided, I made a decision. I settled in my heart that my healing was more important than my dignity, my privacy or the opinions of others. I resolved that I would allow myself to cry whenever I needed to, wherever I was and whoever was looking.

I remember the times I would sit on the tube train travelling home from work with tears trickling down my face as I looked through my little photo album. If I was in a meeting with clients, I would simply excuse myself and retreat to the corridor for five minutes before returning. My handbag and face powder were close at hand so that I could quickly cover my tear-stained cheeks. I may have felt stupid from time to time yet my heart was slowly but surely healing. My tears helped release my grief.

Don't cry

Unfortunately, a common reaction when people are weeping, even when they are children, is to say, "Please don't cry." I don't know why we so readily try to shut down the emotions of others. Perhaps it is because we find it too painful to witness the unrestrained sadness of those we care about. Sometimes, I think it's because we need a good cry too, but we don't want to let go.

Equally, why is it that we feel the need to apologise to people around us when we cry? Time and time again when I'm ministering to hurting people, they will hold back their emotions and then suddenly break. As they cry, they say, "I'm so sorry!" and I always respond, "What for?" I believe that crying is a necessary outlet for any healthy man or woman. He doesn't weep very often, but I'm glad to have a strong husband who is not afraid to cry when he needs to.

Men who cry

In the Bible, many men of God shed tears; Joseph wept bitterly and loudly on many occasions; Jeremiah poured out his heart before the Lord and was known as the weeping prophet; David soaked his bed from crying all night long; Jesus wept when he saw the pain of Martha and Mary; and Paul wept when he said goodbye for the last time to his Ephesian brothers. Let's look at the emotional lives of two of those Bible heroes.

Joseph was betrayed, abandoned, enslaved, falsely accused and imprisoned. It was all because of the jealousy and cruelty of his own flesh and blood. How did he manage to come through thirteen years of terrible suffering to fulfil his destiny? The wounds of our former lives can prevent us possessing the promises of God if they are left to fester and infect our hearts. We get a great insight into Joseph's private life when we look at his reunion with his brothers. He wept his way through it.

Joseph kept a soft heart all those years and learned how to release a myriad of emotions through crying. Joseph wept seven times during that reunion. That's a lot of tears. I believe that the Lord is showing us an important key to healing and freedom. It's a lesson for us all – fathers, mothers, sons, daughters, men, women, leaders. Sometimes, Joseph withdrew from the crowd and cried privately, away from the glare of public attention. Often his tears stained his cheeks:

> ***"Now his heart yearned for his brother, so Joseph made haste and sought somewhere to weep. And he went into his chamber and wept there. Then he washed his face and came out." Genesis 43:30-31***

On other occasions, he cried so loudly that anyone nearby could hear him as he released great depths of emotion:

> ***"He wept aloud and the Egyptians and the house of Pharaoh heard it." Genesis 45:2***

As he wept, he would hug and kiss those he loved and those who had hurt him:

> ***"Then he fell on his brother Benjamin's neck and wept, and Benjamin wept on his neck." Genesis 45:14***

> ***"Moreover he kissed all his brothers and wept over them, and after that his brothers talked with him." Genesis 45:15***

He also wept (and no doubt received great healing) in the arms of his father. I can testify that there is no better place than our Heavenly Father's arms to release tears:

> ***"So Joseph made ready his chariot and went up to Goshen to meet his father Israel; and he presented himself to him, and fell on his face and wept on his neck a good time." Genesis 46:29***

When I went through my healing season, I was blessed to have a wonderful, caring and understanding husband. Sometimes as I sat in the presence of God, telling Him about the things that had hurt me, I would cry in the arms of my husband. At other times, I would pour out my heart and my tears before my Daddy God alone. Tears certainly aren't the evidence of healing, but they are almost always part of the process.

If you have struggled to express sadness or disappointment, I encourage you to ask the Holy Spirit to show you why. Go back to the lesson we learned from Rebekah, Isaac's wife, in chapter three. After twenty years of disappointment and barrenness, God answered Isaac's prayers and Rebekah received her miracle pregnancy. But things weren't as they should have been so the Bible says she went to God in prayer and asked Him why:

"If all is well, then why am I like this?" Genesis 25:22b

There have been many occasions when I have reacted wrongly to life's circumstances. I have felt intimidated by leaders, insecure around successful people, worried about the reactions of relatives and so on. Now, if my reaction is anything other than that of a secure and healed person, I go straight to God in prayer and ask Him why. I don't make excuses for myself. I get to the root of it and ask God to deal with me or heal me – whichever is necessary.

I suggest you develop the same habit in life. God will reveal how the events of your life have affected the way you react in a whole host of situations. If you find it difficult to cry - a normal bodily function - ask the Holy Spirit to show you why and then ask Him to set you free to release the emotions of your heart.

King David was another man who knew how to weep. The Psalms are full of his tears. David cried his way through abandonment, betrayal and many disappointments. He would weep before the Lord as he received his healing. I am sure it was one of the keys to his intimate relationship with God.

"All night I make my bed swim; I drench my couch with my tears... The Lord has heard the voice of my weeping." Psalm 6:2-3, 6, 8

It's alright for them, but why should I cry?

If we keep pain locked up inside, we will remain bound. However, if we pour out our hearts before the Lord and allow tears to fall, we can be set free. It's important that He is the recipient of our tears because when we cry before Him, with our eyes fixed on Jesus, He will release His healing power into our lives. If we cry alone, our tears release pain, but they won't necessarily bring restoration.

> ***"They did not cry out to Me with their heart when they wailed..." Hosea 7:14***

When we pour out our hearts before the Lord, He receives our tears and will release His restoration power into our lives. Our tears are also precious to God. The Bible says in Psalm 56:8 that He puts them in a bottle and keeps them.

As you free the words trapped deep inside, it will help you to release the tears you never cried. Often words are the cork in the bottle and tears are the wine within. Once the words come out, the tears will fall. When we pour out our words and tears before Him in faith, we can be assured that He will release His healing power into our lives. Pain is always better out than in. The release brings relief and eventually joy. The sooner we weep, the sooner we can laugh and seal the healing work of God in our hearts.

> ***"Blessed are you who weep now for you shall laugh." Luke 6:21b***

Prayer

Lord God,

I thank You that You have given me a way to empty my soul of hurt and sadness. I ask You to unblock my emotions so that I can cry real tears of healing. I bring every disappointment and distress to You and ask You to help me release all my pent-up feelings. I want to be whole, I want to be free and I want to laugh so I open the door of my heart to Your healing power. Lord, come and heal me, I pray.

In Jesus' name,

Amen

Chapter 8

Jesus is my healer

It doesn't take long in this imperfect world for someone to do something that deeply wounds you. Pain makes us react. If you suffered a nasty cut on your leg, it would be agony if someone prodded the tender area. Similarly, we know if we are hurt emotionally through our reactions to other people. A whole host of responses are evidence of buried pain.

It might be jealousy when others succeed, insecurity around high achievers, the need to be affirmed by people in authority or the yearning to be recognized when we do well. Pain produces issues.

Why doesn't everyone get healed?

I have ministered to people who have acknowledged all of this, faced the pain buried deep within and embraced the healing process. However, they have limped away, only partially restored. Why is it that some people who have gone through terrible trauma get healed relatively easily and others remain weighed down by their past?

Well, I pray that this book will help many who have struggled to get healed. I believe there are many factors which affect our ability to receive liberty from the Lord.

But before we go any further, there are three 'healing aids' which I want you to know about because I believe they are vital to your journey to wholeness.

1. Focus

One of the traps of the enemy against hurting people is to skew their focus. He will either try to take you into total denial about your wounds so that you refuse to admit you have been damaged. Alternatively, he will try to get you to focus on yourself too much. It is always helpful to remember that there is someone worse off than you. It will help to choke out self-pity.

Shortly after my two year old daughter died in 2000, I saw a news feature about the devastating draught in Somalia. A reporter described a father who had walked eighteen miles to get water for his dehydrated daughter. Just before he reached a well, she died in his arms. Seeing the hopelessness of his situation helped me to remember that people all over the world were experiencing loss like mine, often in far worse circumstances. It put my pain in context.

I recommend that you remember the needs of others when you are suffering yourself. The enemy wants to keep you exclusively focused on yourself. While your focus is only on *your* pain, your problems will appear larger and overwhelming. When you concentrate on Jesus, His infinite power to heal you, and you remember the needs of others, your faith can grow.

> ***"Fix your eyes on Jesus, the author and finisher of our faith..." Hebrews 12:2***

Let us look at the woman with the issue of blood in Mark chapter 5. She had suffered for twelve years and lost everything. At that time, when a woman was bleeding she was considered unclean. This lady had been unclean in the eyes of the world for over a decade. She would almost certainly have lived in solitude during this time. Although she had once been rich, she had spent all her money on ineffective treatments and was now poor as well as ill. Her issue was blood and she knew she needed help. She knew she had to focus on Jesus.

> ***"For she said, "If only I may touch His clothes, I shall be made well." Mark 5:28***

It is very important that as you seek God for restoration, you remember that it is Jesus who is able to heal you. This book will take you through vital steps that will help you to release the pain of the past. However, you will only become whole if the focus of your journey is Jesus. He is your anchor, your helper, your confidant, your counsellor, your partner, your healer, your faithful friend.

2. Hope – the anchor of your soul

Facing the truth can be very difficult. I remember feeling vulnerable for about six months as God took me through my own healing process. During that period, I was painfully aware of the wounds of my heart, the people who had unwittingly hurt me and the memories that were being upturned. Facing pain can be overwhelming if we don't have our eye on the prize – total restoration.

> ***"O Israel, hope in the Lord!" Psalm 130:7***

Hope is confidently expecting that God will do what He has promised to do. It's the assurance that there is an end in sight that is brighter and better. I remember the one thing that kept me on God's operating table was the promise that when I was healed, I would be able to bring healing to the multitudes. I had a picture in my heart of my promise and my destiny.

> ***"Blessed is the man whose strength is in you, whose heart is set on pilgrimage*** **(which means moving on)** ***as they pass through the valley of Baca*** **(which means weeping)** ***they make it a spring; the rain also covers it with pools. They go from strength to strength; each one appears before God in Zion." Psalm 84:5***

Healing is something you pass through on your way to restoration and fulfilment. It will be really important as you allow God to minister to you that you hold onto your own promise of wholeness. Perhaps it's the picture of you as a great father or mother; maybe it's the vision of you as a wonderful husband or a loving wife; possibly it's the hope of God using you to help others or simply the promise of a happier life. If you don't yet have a vision of yourself when you've been healed, ask the Holy Spirit to paint a picture in your mind's eye. Ask Him to show you what your life will be like when you are whole. Ask Him to give you a promise from scripture and then hold onto it with all your strength, knowing the days ahead will be greater than your past.

> ***"There is hope in your future..." Jeremiah 31:17***

Whatever you are believing God for, remember to keep your eyes on the ultimate goal and on God's ability.

Healing is what God does, not what we do. And what He will do for one, He is always ready and willing to do for another.

"This hope we have as an anchor of the soul, both sure and steadfast..." Hebrews 6:19

This verse assures us that hope keeps us stable and steady. Hope anchors our soul - that is, our mind, will and emotions. It means that however difficult it gets, as long as we keep the hope of a positive future with Jesus at the forefront of our thoughts, we can remain strong even in the roughest storms. Remember that healing is God's promise to us from His Word and His Word is His bond.

3. Your Faith has made you well

Our relationship with God is entirely based on faith. We walk by faith and not by sight. We are called to "Imitate those who by faith and patience inherit the promises." (Hebrew 6:12)

We will receive God's healing power as we believe God's Word. So what does God's Word say about the healing of our hearts? Let us look first at the very scripture that described Jesus' mission on earth:

"The Spirit of the Lord God is upon Me for He has anointed Me to preach good tidings to the poor; He has sent Me to bind up the broken-hearted, to proclaim liberty to the captives and the opening of the prison door to those who are bound; to proclaim the acceptable year of the Lord, and the day of vengeance of our God; to comfort all who mourn, to console those who mourn in

Zion, to give them beauty for ashes, the oil of joy for mourning, the garment of praise for heaviness." Isaiah 61:1-3

As well as bringing salvation to the lost and healing to sick bodies, Jesus came to bind up the broken-hearted and set captives free. He died to bring comfort to those who are mourning. A large part of Jesus' mission was to heal the wounded heart. He came, lived, died and was raised from the dead that we might be saved, healed, delivered and completely restored. It was at the cross that the final price was paid.

"Surely He has borne our griefs and carried our sorrows... He was wounded for our transgressions, He was bruised for our iniquities; the punishment for our peace was laid upon Him, and by His stripes we are healed." Isaiah 53:4-5

In His suffering, Jesus secured your healing. He was rejected so that you could know acceptance. He was hated so that you could know love. He was mocked so that when you were humiliated or bullied, you could be affirmed. He was abused and beaten so that you could receive healing from physical, emotional and sexual abuse. The price has been paid and by faith you can receive everything He bought for you on the cross. When you come to Jesus in faith, believing He is faithful and holding onto His Word, He will heal.

"...He who promised is faithful" Hebrew 10:23

He will take you on a journey of truth that will increase your capacity to love as well as bring you healing. He will set you free so that others can be delivered. They key is to keep your eyes on Jesus the whole way through your healing process. He has the power and the desire to heal you.

> ***"I will restore health to you and heal you of your wounds." Jeremiah 30:17***

> ***"The crooked places shall be made straight and the rough places smooth and (then) the glory of the Lord shall be revealed..." Isaiah 40:4-5***

We obtain the healing of the soul in the same way that we receive the healing of the body: by faith in Jesus Christ. The Bible tells us that Abraham's wife Sarah overcame decades of disappointment to get her promise. The book of Hebrews gives us a wonderful insight into how she did this. We know from God's Word that He is faithful, but how much do we really believe that to be true in our own lives? The Bible says:

> ***"By faith <u>Sarah herself also received strength</u> to conceive seed and she bore a child when she was past the age, because <u>she judged Him faithful who had promised</u>." Hebrews 11:11***

Look carefully at this verse. Sarah herself - not Abraham, or her leader, pastor or counsellor - actively chose to receive strength from God to conceive. There is strength available to you too. The Bible tells us to, "Put on strength", in Isaiah 52:1, "Be strong", in Joshua 1:6 and, "March on in strength", in Judges 5:21. Doubtless, there are times when God is our strength because we have none left (Psalm 37:39), but it is always best to let God determine that. Take God's Word, which is His seed, and plant it in your heart by reading, believing and confessing healing scriptures. However tough things get, believe His Word.

The other lesson we learn from this verse is that Sarah chose to take the Lord's promise personally and to believe in His faithfulness to her. I encourage you to make that choice today. Judge Jesus as faithful. Open your heart and believe that He will do for you what He has done for others. Take God's Word to heart and start trusting Him for your complete restoration.

> ***"He heals the broken-hearted and binds up their wounds." Psalm 147:3***

I have seen people weep as they remember painful events. However, without faith, our tears are merely a release of pent-up emotion. Although that in itself is incredibly helpful, releasing one's feelings is not enough to heal a broken heart. That requires the intervention of a miracle-working God.

> ***"...I am the Lord who heals you." Exodus 15:26***

After Jesus' power was released in the life of the woman with the issue of blood, He spoke some very important words to her:

> ***"Daughter, your faith has made you well. Go in peace and be healed of your affliction." Mark 5:34***

It was her faith in Jesus that released His power. Focus on Jesus, keep the hope of a better future alive and plant the seed of God's Word in your heart. You will surely be made whole.

Prayer

Lord Jesus,

I thank You that You are my healer. I fix my eyes on You because I know that You are the One who is able to restore. You are the Way to abundant life.

Father, I thank you for the dreams and promises which You have given me about my life. I know that as You heal me, I will become ready for all that You have in store for me. My hope is in You, not in any process or book. And hope is the anchor that will keep me secure through the storm.

Lord, I put my trust in You. As I meditate on Your word and Your promises, I thank You that my faith will grow. You bore my griefs on the cross and You carried my sorrows so that I can be made whole. By Your wounds, I am healed.

Thank you, Lord, that You are with me, leading me to wholeness and peace.

I give You praise and glory.

In Jesus' name,

Amen

Chapter 9

The pivot

A notable preacher once said that refusing to forgive someone is like drinking poison in the hope that the other person will die. The sad reality is that the only one who really gets hurt is you. Forgiveness is something we need to do for ourselves and for the love of God, not necessarily for those who have hurt us.

Unforgiveness has a knack of keeping you bound to the people and pain of the past. That makes it very difficult to get healed and move on. By contrast, forgiveness is one of the doors to healing. Sometimes we need to receive a measure of healing in order to release forgiveness, but unless we let go of the wrongs done to us, we can't lay hold of a brighter future. And staying bound is by no means the greatest penalty of unforgiveness.

What's the problem?

> ***"And whenever you stand praying, if you have anything against anyone, forgive him that your heavenly Father may also forgive you your trespasses. But if you do not forgive, neither will your Father in heaven forgive your trespasses." Mark 11:25-26***

Scripture is painfully clear. If we don't forgive others, God won't forgive us. Most of us ask God for forgiveness on a daily or weekly basis. As His Spirit convicts us of our wrongs, we ask the Lord to wipe them away and He faithfully does this. We bathe to keep our bodies clean and we rely on God's cleansing mercy to wash our hearts. In order to enjoy God's immeasurable gift of grace, we need to give a gift of grace to others: forgiveness.

This might sound harsh, but let me reassure you: it is one of the kindest principles in scripture. You see, our loving heavenly Father knows how badly bitterness can damage us. The devil always tries to convince us that unforgiveness is our right and seeking vengeance is our due. He deceives us into believing that holding grudges will punish those who hurt us. Satan also propagates the lie that forgiveness is one of the most difficult duties to discharge. It's like doing anything for the first time. After the initial step into the unknown, it becomes easier and it is one of the greatest blessings available to us.

Harbouring a grudge is very destructive. When we allow unforgiveness to fester, it will take hold and burrow down into our lives. A root of bitterness is formed in our hearts, producing fruits such as resentment and spite. The Bible warns us that this situation can cause emotional and physical problems.

> ***"For I see that you are <u>poisoned</u> by bitterness and bound by iniquity." Acts 8:23***

If poison gets into your bloodstream, it can cause your organs to shut down and eventually kill you. When it is left to pollute and linger, bitterness has the same effect on our spirit and soul. We cannot flourish and allow bitterness to remain in our hearts.

> ***"Resentment destroys the fool..." Job 5:2***

Resentment is when we feel bitter or indignant about another person. We may resent them being blessed when they have done or said things that have hurt us. Really, it is foolish to hold resentments. It will eventually destroy us on the inside.

> ***"Looking carefully lest anyone should fall short of the grace of God; lest any root of bitterness springing up causes trouble and by this many become defiled." Hebrews 12:15***

Bitterness causes trouble. It poisons and defiles us as well as the people close to us. It risks placing us outside the reach of the grace of God. I believe bitterness is the very opposite of grace. It is a toxic mix of unforgiveness and judgement. When we are in unforgiveness, we are in judgement. We are saying by our heart's actions, "You should pay for your wrong. You don't deserve compassion or kindness." We are wanting others to pay for their sins and demanding justice for wrongdoing. When we stand in judgement against another human being, there are troubling consequences:

> ***"Do not judge or you too will be judged. For in the same way you judge others, you will be judged and with the measure you use, it will be measured to you." Matthew 7:1-2***

If we judge others, we will also be judged. When we sow judgement, we will reap judgment. I don't know about you, but I depend on the marvellous mercy of God. I need His mercy to cover my many mistakes and His grace to shine on me despite my shortcomings and weaknesses.

I covet the generosity of heart and goodwill of my family, friends, church members and so on. When I fail or slip up (as I often do,) I seek their understanding and forgiveness. I need my husband to forgive me when I mess up. I want my children to show mercy when I'm short-tempered or impatient. I look to my team to be gracious when I get things wrong. I consider walking in mercy and forgiveness to be very important for a happy life.

So how do we do it?

I have had to forgive many people over the years: family, husband, doctors, leaders, church members, friends and so on. In fact, I was probably forgiving on a weekly basis as I went through my healing process and I have never stopped. It's not always that others have actually wronged me. However, if I *feel* wronged then I need to let go of it.

Everything that we do in Christ must be from the heart. Praying prayers that don't reflect the cry of the heart probably don't get any further than your bedroom ceiling. In the same way, when we forgive, we need to forgive from the heart. The Bible says that unless we do this, God won't forgive us. It's what goes on in our heart

- and not only what we say with our lips - that counts before God.

> ***"So My heavenly Father will also do to you if each of you, from his heart, does not forgive his brother..." Matthew 18:35***

For many people, forgiveness will be quite a process. When your heart has been broken or your life destroyed by the actions, words, abuse, failings or behaviour of someone you trusted, forgiveness doesn't happen instantly.

Sometimes, we look at the scale of the injustice or wrongdoing and feel as though we are letting cruel or abusive people off the hook by forgiving them their trespasses. In reality, our unforgiveness doesn't hurt them anyway. It only hurts us. Unforgiveness keeps us bound to those who have hurt us the most, whereas forgiveness sets us free.

After our daughter died, it soon became clear that the doctor caring for her was guilty of serious neglect. If our little one had been given a simple dose of intravenous antibiotics on arrival at hospital, she would be with us today. In fact, our child had to wait nine hours before she was given a ten dollar injection that could have saved her life.

We had to forgive that doctor quickly. We knew we couldn't bear the weight of bitterness as well as the pain of bereavement. Although it was difficult at first, before God, we released that clinician for her part in our daughter's death. For the sake of integrity, and to protect the lives of other children, we lodged an official complaint which led to the introduction of much tighter procedures. But we did not hold any grudge in our hearts. On the contrary, we often prayed for that doctor and asked God to bless her.

Releasing forgiveness brings relief and refreshment. If bitterness is poison, as Acts 8:23 says, then forgiveness is a deep cleansing agent. It's like laying down a lifetime of senseless struggle and strain.

I encourage you to forgive those who have hurt you right now. If you aren't sure if you have forgiven or not, it's always better to be sure. Go to God in prayer and tell Him who you are forgiving and why. It will be really important that you are specific and that you tell the Lord exactly what they did and how it hurt you. Then tell the Lord that you forgive them. Let it go and say that you do not want God to hold their sin against them anymore. There may be many people and many events that you need to forgive. Take the time to be specific and to be real.

Such love

As Stephen was stoned to death by people who hated him with such venom that they gnashed their teeth, he said: "Lord do not charge them with this sin." Acts 7:60

What was it in the heart of Stephen that enabled him to show such forgiveness at a time of dreadful suffering? I believe he understood that he needed the mercy and love of God himself like never before, so he knew he had to give mercy and love to others.

One of the best ways to seal forgiveness is to pray for the people who hurt you. Like Stephen, ask God for His mercy to be poured out into their lives. Ask Him to heal them, restore them and increase them. The more you bless them – in every area of their lives – the more you will be set free from anger and filled with new joy.

> ***"Bless those who curse you, do good to those who hate you and pray for those who spitefully use you and persecute you..." Matthew 5:44***

What a guy!

Joseph's life is among my favourite stories in scripture. He suffered terribly at the hands of those who were nearest and dearest to him. He had every reason to be bitter towards his brothers. But Joseph had a destiny to fulfil and a dream to accomplish. He knew he had to guard his heart because fulfilment depended on it. He could not afford to hold anger against anyone, not even those who hurt him the most.

In chapter 7, I talked of the importance of keeping a picture of your future in front of your eyes. Let hope anchor you through the storm. It worked for Joseph and I know it can work for you. I believe Joseph kept his dream alive as he was sold into slavery and thrown into prison. He chose to remember God's promises and he guarded his heart for the sake of his destiny. It is really important that you forgive so that you can be restored and fulfil your potential. You need to forgive to be free to live life to the full.

But where do I draw the line?

There is a difference between forgiveness and trust. Some people get caught up in this one, worrying that if they forgive, they will walk into the same traps of the past and be hurt and betrayed all over again. Forgiveness is a free gift that we give because God has forgiven us. However, trust is earned.

The life of Joseph demonstrates the distinction. When he was reunited with his brothers, it was obvious that Joseph had forgiven them a long time beforehand. He was moved to tears at seeing them again. If he had been bitter, he would have been hard-hearted, probably gloating in their poverty and lording it over them with his pomp and prosperity. Instead, Joseph was generous and kind. But although he had forgiven them, he didn't yet trust them. They needed to earn this first.

Don't make them grovel

Seventeen years after Joseph's reunion with his family, their father, Jacob, died. His brothers were afraid that Joseph might now seize his chance to take revenge. They wondered if his restraint had only been for the sake of their father. Perhaps he had harboured hatred all these years, waiting for the opportunity to exact vengeance. Terrified, they went to Joseph and asked him to forgive them.

> ***"His brothers also went and fell down before his face and they said, 'Behold we are your servants.' Joseph said to them, 'Do not be afraid, for am I in the place of God? As for you, you meant evil against me but God meant it for***

good, in order to bring it about as it is this day, to save many people alive." Genesis 50:18-20

I am pretty sure that if that had been me, I would have revelled in that moment. Even if I had dealt with resentment, I would have seen this as an opportunity to make them squirm for their sins (just for a little while) and to remind them of their wrongdoing.

Not Joseph. He saw God as the only one worthy to judge. He had been betrayed, abandoned, enslaved, falsely accused and imprisoned, but he did not believe that he had the right to judge anyone. It was thirty years since they had sold him as a slave, seventeen years since they were first reunited and still Joseph was soft-hearted towards them:

"And Joseph wept when they spoke to him." Genesis 50:17b.

Perhaps he was receiving the completion of his healing. I know that when we show mercy and when we reach out, God is able to use our open heart to minister to us. When we sow love, we reap love. When we sow grace, we reap grace. Joseph showed mercy to his brothers when he had the opportunity to demand justice. As a result, he received a new ministry of healing and reconciliation. Through his ability to forgive and love, he became the healer of his brothers also:

"'But as for you, you meant evil against me, but God meant it for good, in order to bring it about as it is this day, to save many people alive. Now therefore, do not be afraid; I will provide for you and your little ones.' And he comforted them and spoke kindly to their hearts." Genesis 50:20-21

As you allow the love of God to soften your heart towards the people who have hurt you the most, it will release kindness, mercy and maybe even a new ministry into your life. Not only will God heal and liberate you, He will use you to bring healing to others. Now that's what I call life in Christ!

PS

If you are struggling in this area, there is a short book that I must recommend, The Importance of Forgiveness by John Arnott. I believe it is one of the very best teachings on this vital subject and I am sure that it will help you to break free.

Prayer

As you pray, be specific and tell God exactly who you are forgiving and why. You may need to repeat this process with several people on several occasions. The important thing is that you get there in the end. It may be hard at first, but soon you will find that it feels good to forgive.

Father God,

I realise that I need to forgive. I ask You for Your help because I want to forgive from the depths of my heart. I want to give forgiveness because I have already received forgiveness from You.

I come to You today and bring (the person's name) to You. I forgive them for every time I have been hurt. I forgive them for rejecting me. I forgive them for ignoring me and my needs. I forgive them for pushing me away. I forgive them for betraying me. I forgive them for using me. I forgive them for lying about me and to me. I forgive them for cheating me. I forgive them for preferring someone else. I forgive them for hurting me (please try and be specific).

I ask You to forgive (the person's name) too and to heal and restore them. And as Your word teaches me, I bless them. I bless their health, I bless their family, I bless the work of their hands and I bless all their relationships.

In Jesus' name, I pray,

Amen

Chapter 10

Breaking the power of hate

"The archers have bitterly grieved him, shot at him and hated him." Genesis 49:23

When you think about Judah in the Bible, what words or thoughts come to mind? Do you think of him as the head of one of the greatest tribes of Israel, an outstanding leader of worship and an ancestor of King David and even Christ? What about Levi? When you think of him, what do you reflect on? Do you see the head of one of the most important tribes of Israel, a priest and minister of God and the great, great, great etc grandfather of Moses and Aaron? Both Judah and Levi were used powerfully in their generation and, following their deaths, their offspring were mighty on the earth. They were serious men of God.

Yet the Bible tells us that this great worship leader and this righteous reverend hated their brother. The blatant favouritism that their father showed to their younger brother, Joseph, deeply wounded these men of destiny. The wounds festered and ultimately produced hate. It was hate that drove Joseph's brothers to beat him, strip him of his coloured robe and sell him into slavery.

The Hebrew word for hate is 'satam' and it means to 'cherish animosity against'. In other words, when we hate, we take delight in our loathing and we harbour animosity. When someone consistently wounds you over months, years or decades, it is possible that hatred can take root. If you have never considered that you have any hatred in your heart, I would like to ask you to invite the Holy Spirit to search your soul.

It's easy to think, "I'm a Christian. I don't hate anyone. Hate's a very strong word and it's not my portion. I'm just hurt and need healing." Well, that might be true but in the Bible, God speaks to His people about hate on many occasions. Good people can end up hating because they are terribly hurt. It is far better for us to face the truth and get delivered than remain in denial because it's difficult to swallow. The truth sets us free.

Jane spent years desperately trying to forgive her sister. She came to God in prayer, time after time, but she was still riddled with resentment. Jane would go home with the best of intentions. Then she would become irritated and even disgusted by the same pattern of behaviour from her sister. Getting away from home would always end up being her priority. Jane really wanted to forgive and walk in love because she wanted to please God.

Jane's issues were deep-seated. From a very young age, her sister had taunted and ridiculed her in front of family, friends and strangers. Things grew worse as Jane reached her teenage years. The humiliation now took place in front of her peers. Her parents had never protected her and she needed significant healing as a young adult. The big obstacle in her life was her relationship with her sister.

It was only when I suggested to Jane that her issue was not unforgiveness but hate that everything became clear. Jane released a lifetime of bitterness as she acknowledged that hate had entered her heart when she was a young child. It wasn't forgiveness that was needed first. It was an exchange at the cross – her hate for God's wonderful love. She still had to forgive and then work out her newfound freedom. However, the root of the problem - which was actually hatred – had been cut.

You can't choose your family

Hate is a very real problem in the body of Christ, especially among family members. The Bible tells us that we must not hold on to hate:

> ***"You shall not hate your brother in your heart." Leviticus 19:17-18***

The New Living Translation reveals what this scripture is trying to teach us:

> ***"Do not nurse hatred in your heart for any of your relatives."***

God wouldn't ask us to deal with hate if it wasn't a fairly common problem. If we don't know whether or not we hate, then we can't deal with it if it's there. If we reach a place of understanding, we can get help from the Lord if it's necessary to remove hate from our hearts.

How do I know if I hate?

We know the symptoms of common illnesses. As a result, doctors can easily diagnose what is wrong with the body and prescribe the correct medicine. In the same way, the Bible tells us the symptoms of hate so that we can recognise the problem and apply the right remedy.

As you read the next few passages, ask the Holy Spirit to expose any root of hatred - towards the living or the dead - which the enemy has tried to hide in your heart. With hate, you would expect to experience most or all of the following attitudes.

1. You can't speak kindly to them – "When his brothers saw that their father loved him more... they hated him and could not speak a kind word to him." Genesis 37:4. When you hate someone, you struggle to speak kindly to them. Antagonism and criticism are on your lips. Good words only come out through gritted teeth and sheer determination. Maybe you want to do the right thing. You plan to be gracious and considerate, but all too often you end up being harsh. You are left feeling disappointed, guilty and frustrated.
2. You like leaving them out – "Your brothers who hate you exclude you." Isaiah 66:5. When you hate someone, you don't want them to be around you. You try to ensure that you're not in the same place as them for very long. If you have to spend time together, you keep the meeting as short as possible and you prefer others to be there too. You enjoy socialising with other family members (if the person you hate is family) when they are excluded. In your heart, you think they deserve to be left out.
3. You hold a grudge – "You shall not hate your brother in your heart... you shall not seek vengeance nor bear any grudge but you shall love your neighbour as yourself."

Leviticus 19:17-18. When you hate someone, you secretly gloat when things don't go well for them. You might pretend that you're sad, but actually you're pleased. On the other hand, if they're experiencing success, you try to undermine their achievements. You hold anger in your heart towards them. You remember the things that they have done which hurt you. When people speak well of them, you recall the behaviour that contradicts that admiration and love.

4. <u>You feel agitated when they are around</u> – "Hatred stirs up strife." Proverbs 10:12. When you are around a person you hate, you find it hard to resist stirring up arguments. You seldom, if ever, agree with their point of view or support their endeavours. You feel prickly and hostile when you see their face or even hear their name.

So what's the problem?

If we harbour hatred, it will harm us and prevent us from moving on with our lives.

> ***"He who hates his brother is in darkness and walks in darkness, and does not know where he is going, because the darkness has blinded his eyes." 1 John 2:11***

I don't know about you, but I want to find out God's will for my life. I want to see what God is doing in the world and what He wants to do in my life. While we hate, it's as though we're walking around wearing a blindfold. Hate switches off God's light in our lives.

When it comes to our parents, the Bible goes even further. A passage in Leviticus 20 shows us how seriously God views hate. There is a register of sins that God thinks are so serious that they deserve death (you must remember that this is the Old Testament, before Jesus shed His blood which is powerful enough to cleanse any sin).

Included in this inventory are incest and bestiality but at the top of the list of wrongs requiring death is cursing one's father or mother (verse 9). This is when we treat our father or mother with contempt, when we dishonour them or discredit them in the sight of others with our words. If you hate your father or mother, it will be all too easy to find yourself cursing them without even realising it.

If you have been rejected, abused, abandoned or wounded in some way by a parent, the devil may try to bury hate and contempt deep in your heart. Satan wants to keep you from the promises of God that are available to those who honour their parents.

The Bible makes two wonderful pledges:

> ***"Honour your father and your mother that (1) your days may be long and that (2) it may be well with you." Exodus 20:12***

The enemy always tries to steal the promises of God from us. He attempts to use legal arguments to shorten our days and to ensure that things don't go well for us. It's not enough for the enemy that you were wounded and crushed. He wants to make sure your life today is a mess and he would love to end it prematurely. That's why he resists the healing process so much. He knows better than anyone that when God heals your heart and you reject hatred, you are on the road to restoration.

Getting rid of hate

Hate is horrible. We were made in the image of God and God is love. Love is what we do best because we were designed to love and not to despise. If you have been holding hate in your heart, it is time to ask the Lord to take it away.

If you realise that you hate – or have hated – your father or mother, now is the chance to deal with it and make sure the devil doesn't attack you anymore.

Perhaps it's not your parents. Maybe you recognise that you have hate in your heart towards someone who has hurt you or a person you once trusted.

God showed me a wonderful way of breaking hate's power. Bring hate to the Lord as an offering. Ask Him to receive the hate in your heart as an act of surrender to His ways and His love. Picture yourself bringing this hate to the cross of Jesus and laying it down there as a sacrifice. At the cross Christ broke its power by His love.

Then ask Him to cleanse your heart from all contempt and dishonour. Repent of any negative words spoken and anything done to repay evil for evil. Ask Him to forgive you for curses spoken, unkind words shared, bad attitudes, evil wishes and grudges. Ask Him to cleanse you of every remnant of hate – He is able!

Now, in exchange for your hate, ask God to pour His unconditional love into your life. Ask Him to fill your heart with His love for those you once hated. Ask for more than enough love for every day. Once you have dealt with hate, it will be so much easier to forgive.

Prayer

Loving Father,

I realise that I have been taken captive by hate. I was deeply hurt and, as a result, hate grew in my heart. I have found it difficult to be kind. I have held grudges. I have willingly excluded those who have hurt me. I have been irritated and on edge around them and I have had enough of it all. I am sorry, Lord, and I repent of every sinful attitude and word. Please forgive me and cleanse me from wrongdoing.

I want to be free from negative emotions towards those who have hurt me. I want to be free from the past. I want to be blameless in Your sight.

So today, I bring my hate to You. I lay it down at Your feet, Lord Jesus, as an offering. I don't want it anymore so please take it away. It's not my portion and You died to break its power. Receive my offering, Lord.

Please fill me now with Your unconditional love. Give me Your love for those people. Give me Your love for everyone. You made me in Your image and You are love. May love grow in my heart daily.

In Jesus' name, I pray,

Amen

Chapter 11

Regrets

When I was ministering in Ghana a few years ago, a young pastor in training asked me a very pertinent question: "What is the one thing in your life that you would do differently if you were given the chance?" It is not easy to render me speechless, but I was silent for quite a while. After all, I had a lot to think about.

What's your greatest regret?

Was my greatest regret the childhood I experienced and the pain and dysfunction in my family? If I'd had a normal upbringing, I would not have been so insecure and inadequate. I would not have tried to find acceptance in all the wrong places.

Was my greatest regret the backslidden life I led at university? No one else was to blame. I messed myself up so much that I entered my marriage years later with far too much baggage. I repeatedly rejected my husband and the impact very nearly crushed him.

Was my greatest regret not getting my daughter to hospital in time? If I had got up in the middle of the night and called an ambulance, she would be here today. But I was gripped with fear and I lay there hoping she would be OK in the morning. She wasn't just my daughter. She was my husband's daughter too and I failed at the time when she was in greatest need. I left it just long enough for the invisible but deadly bacteria to spread throughout her tiny frame before she received medical help.

Was my greatest regret that the doctor at the accident and emergency room did not take her condition more seriously? The doctor carried out tests and discovered a serious infection, but didn't give her antibiotics until it was too late. Our little girl was at hospital for nine long hours before she was given any medicine. She died as a result of multiple organ failure at the tender age of two.

Regret is a terribly destructive emotion. It makes us recoil from the memories of the past, leaving us feeling helpless, disappointed and often riddled with guilt and shame. It is very difficult to live with regret so we turn our face away from the cause and avoid the facts.

> ***"Oh, that you were like my brother... I would not be despised." Song of Songs 8:1***

The Shulamite struggled with regret. This verse shows how she wished King Solomon had been around while she was growing up. "If only my brothers had not abused me. If only my parents had protected me, I wouldn't be in this mess." Her regret is directed towards others. "Why did they do that to me? Why couldn't I have had decent, caring siblings and parents who paid attention to me?"

Job is another Bible character who felt immense remorse. He reflected on how his life was before tragedy hit and longed to turn the clock back.

> ***"Oh that I were in months past, as in the days when God watched over me; when His lamp shone upon me and when by His light I walked through darkness. Just as I was in the days of my prime... when my children were around me; when my steps were bathed with cream and the rock poured out rivers of oil for me." Job 29: 2-6***

Similarly, King David wished he could escape from his suffering by re-winding his life:

> ***"My heart is severely pained within me...So I said 'O that I had wings like a dove! I would fly away and be at rest. Indeed, I would wander far off and remain in the wilderness. I would hasten my escape from the windy storm and the tempest.'" Psalm 55:4-8***

If these great men of God were taunted by regret and remorse, you should not be surprised if the same thing happens to you. How many times are God's precious people harassed by the enemy, who constantly points to a time when things were better, or to big mistakes which they made?

I remember being tormented by regret after our daughter died. "Why didn't I get up in the night and go to the hospital?" I knew my little girl was very sick, but I was afraid. I was worried about what my husband would say if I woke him. He was normally the one who would rush to get medical help.

There I was, in the early hours of the morning, frozen by confusion and anxiety. I knew in my heart that my sweetheart needed help. However, fear bound me so I didn't get her to the hospital in time. When she needed me most, I wasn't there for her and my precious angel died before her second birthday. I couldn't properly face that regret, so most of the time I denied it.

On the other hand, the hospital's failure was easier to deal with. If Naomi had been given antibiotics on arrival, she would be here today. "Why did *that* doctor have to be there? And why didn't she do her job? If only things had been different..."

I have met many people who have struggled over years and even decades to come to terms with regret. Women who became bitter over abortions, men who lost huge sums of money on the stock market, alcoholics who drank their lives down the drain, single women who got pregnant through a one-night stand after years of waiting in purity, husbands who reaped the catastrophic consequences of an extra-marital affair, people whose childhoods were robbed by sexual abuse. The list is endless.

Our miracle-working God

However, our God is a miracle-working God. One of the most remarkable things about our life in Christ is His ability to turn our circumstances around. The Bible says that God literally 'turned' Job's captivity. In other words, in every area where Job had been stripped of dignity, possessions and loved ones, God ultimately blessed him with greater happiness than he had known before disaster hit.

In Isaiah, God promises that He will take away our shame and give us honour instead. When we repent of the mistakes of the past, He will pour twice as many blessings into our life. Through the wondrous ways of God, the devil is confounded and we can experience true restoration.

> ***"Comfort, yes, comfort My people!' says your God. 'Speak comfort to the heart of Jerusalem, and cry out to her, that her warfare is ended, that her iniquity is pardoned, for she has received from the Lord's hand double for all her sins." Isaiah 40:1-2***

I am continually amazed at God's far-reaching love. I find it incredible that He would cover my mistakes, remove my sin, heal my wounds and promise me a life where I am clothed with His honour and lavished with His goodness.

> ***"Instead of your shame you shall have double honour, and instead of confusion, they shall rejoice in their portion (their circumstances). Therefore in their land they shall possess double; everlasting joy shall be theirs." Isaiah 61:7***

After a severe storm, tragedy or trauma, we can sometimes imagine that our best prospect is survival. But out of God's infinite mercy and His great favour towards us, He promises so much more - He promises us everlasting joy.

Probably one of the most incredible scriptures in the Bible is God's promise that He will turn *any* and *every* situation around:

> ***"We know that all things work together for good to those who love God, to those who are called according to His purpose." Romans 8:28***

If you look at the Greek in this verse, you will discover it says that God causes all things - every trial, tragedy, hardship, hurt, mistake or mess-up - to work out somehow for our good. If you grasp this scripture, you can be set free from regret.

The key is believing that God is able to do it. It is time to lay down the regret of the past. Maybe you need to stop punishing yourself for sins that the Father has already punished Jesus for. By not forgiving yourself, you are denying the power of the cross. You should lay down remorse. Accept that you have made some mistakes, but acknowledge that God is the Master Restorer.

If you give Him your regret and choose to believe His Word that He can and He will turn around your mistakes for good, then the rest of your life will begin again. Take Romans 8:28 and declare it over your life and the lives of your loved ones. God specialises in weakness and failure. He can turn your mess into a message that will minister to many.

> ***"So I will restore to you the years that the swarming locust has eaten, the crawling locust, the consuming locust and the chewing locust, My great army which I sent among you. You shall eat in plenty and be satisfied, and praise the name of the Lord your God who has dealt wondrously with you; and My people shall never be put to shame." Joel 2:25-26***

When you refuse regret and receive the mercy, love and favour of God - despite what has happened - you are destroying the devil's plan for your demise.

Eventually, I answered that young Ghanaian man who asked me about regret. I told him that there was nothing that I regretted. I went on to tell him that I had seen the goodness of God bring healing, restoration and joy into every area of my life. I honestly don't regret anything anymore. I depend on the love and mercy of God. I know that He will always turn every trouble in my life around so that mistakes and disasters become the beginning of a testimony.

The same God who healed, comforted, delivered and forgave me has also used the worst circumstances of my life to bring hope to many as I have ministered at churches, conferences and retreats. Truly, God has worked every situation that I have been through for my good and the good of others. No wonder the devil tries to keep us choked with regret!

No more shame

The vital step is believing God's Word. If you carry shame, you need to give it to Jesus in exchange for His honour. Bring it to Him in prayer and tell Him that you don't want to walk around ashamed anymore because He has already paid the price for you. Ask Him to take it away and to give you His honour instead. You are a better testimony when you let go of shame and receive His glory.

> ***"They looked to Him and were radiant, and their faces were not ashamed." Psalm 34:5***

> ***"Do not fear, for you will not be ashamed; nor be disgraced, for you will not be put to shame. For you will***

forget the shame of your youth and will not remember the reproach of your widowhood anymore." Isaiah 54:4

It's only the devil who tells you that shame is your portion. If God says you don't have to be ashamed, I think you would do very well to believe it.

Letting go

Take some time to recall the circumstances you most regret and bring God's Word into those memories. Tell yourself, and the devil, that God will turn those situations around for your good and that of others. Choose to believe that even your darkest memories will bring glory to Him. Stop running away from the difficulties of the past and instead take the power of God's Word to them. Tell those memories that God will turn them around for your good.

Let us look back at the Shulamite. The King loved to see her face. He never wished her cheeks had been protected from the sun's harmful rays. He loved her just as she was. He didn't regret the disfigurement or wish she had never been abused because he had a vision of her healing. He could see that the scars of her childhood would become evidence of God's healing power in her life.

"Your cheeks are lovely..." Song of Songs 1:10

The day will come when your past no longer pains you. Instead, it will paint a picture of God's healing and restoring power. You don't need to regret anything. God is able to turn it all around. You don't have to be ashamed of the past. God will clothe you with dignity and honour.

Prayer

Father God,

I have regretted too many things for too long. I realise that You are able to turn around the events of my life so that they become a testimony. I give all my regrets to You today (*be specific and tell God exactly what you are talking about*) and I choose to believe your Word that You will cause even the difficult and dark times in my life to work together for my good and the good of those I love.

I trust You and I believe Your promise to me. I lay down all shame and remorse. I refuse to be ashamed anymore. Instead, I receive the honour that You clothe me with. You are able to turn the very events that caused me to mourn into a source of joy.

Thank you, Lord, for your amazing favour!

In Jesus' name, I pray,

Amen.

Chapter 12

Why?

At the time of our daughter's death, my husband and I were pastoring a small but growing church in London. We certainly weren't perfect but we were serving the Lord with all of our hearts and had given our lives to the ministry. Our little girl was a bright, healthy child with a beautiful smile. Naomi means 'our delight' and that's exactly what she was. So when she was tragically torn from us, our lives were shattered. One day she was running around a local shopping centre with my husband and the next day she was fighting a losing battle for her life.

At the hospital, we stood in faith. We were praising, praying and believing God that she would recover. We took God at His Word. After she died, we gathered a small team of prayer warriors to believe with us that she would be raised from the dead. But she never even stirred.

After I recovered from shock, the question on my lips and ringing in my mind was, "why?" Why had God, the Creator of heaven and earth, and our faithful Healer, allowed our little girl to die? Never for one moment did I think that it was God's will for her to die. He is not the author of sin or sickness. His plans for us are always for good and not for evil, to give us a hope and a bright future (Jeremiah 29:11). And I knew then, as I do now, that my Lord is a miracle-working God who can heal every disease.

This question perturbed me and I found myself coming back to the same concerns again and again. I thought that if I could just find out why she died, then I would be able to move on. I don't know what you have gone through, but perhaps your suffering has led you to ask questions. "Why would a loving God allow this to happen? What did I do wrong? Why me? Why us? Why her?"

I would watch other parents: those who chain-smoked with their children by their side; those who let their little ones play around dangerous staircases; those who shouted and cursed at their sons and daughters. And none of it made sense.

The premature death of loved ones often causes people to ask why it happened. Abuse can lead its victims to wonder what they did wrong. Divorce, separation and betrayal make many desperate to find out why their partners rejected them. Life often deals out difficult trials. When it does, we can be left reeling and wondering why.

Getting an answer

I sought God for an answer for several months because these questions were dominating my thoughts. In my quest, I came across the testimony of an American lady who had also lost her daughter. Through her story and my own study, God spoke to me...

I learned that the word why - along with other questioning terms like who, what, when and where - is rooted in the Hebrew word for chaos. I realised that while I was seeking an answer, it would only lead to confusion and remorse. Then God started to show me that even if He were to tell me why, the explanation would never be sufficient. If Jesus came back to earth at that time and explained why Naomi had died, there is nothing that He could have said that would have been a good enough reason.

There is something else I learned. In the book of Job, the Bible says that when God restored him after his tragedy, Job received a double portion of everything: double the number of cows, double the number of sheep and so on. But, Job fathered exactly the same number of children again: seven sons and three daughters. Ten children died during his catastrophe and he raised ten children when he was restored.

What God revealed about this was beautiful. It's not that He valued cattle more than Job's sons and daughters. When cattle die, they are gone. However, when his children died, they simply moved to a better place. He hadn't actually lost his first children. They had simply gone to heaven and were waiting to be reunited with him in the fullness of time.

Job *did* get a double portion of children. He had twenty by the time he went to be with the Lord. I realised that I needed an eternal perspective. Naomi hadn't been lost, she had merely moved on.

The turning point

In understanding these things, I made a monumental decision. I decided to lay down the question of why. I decided to give up any right I felt I had to an explanation. I went to God and said, "I don't know why Naomi had to die, but I don't need to know anymore. I surrender my right to an answer and instead, Lord, I ask You to heal my heart." That proved to be one of the most important decisions I took in the journey to restoration.

If you had asked me before Naomi died if I could recover if I lost her, I would have told you, "No, never. She is too precious." Yet, after I gave up on why, when I laid down my right to answers and relinquished my need to know, God started to heal me.

It's all too easy for the enemy to bind our pain to our chests if we demand an explanation. It keeps us looking backwards. When I chose a future instead of the past, God was able to make me whole.

If you have struggled with asking why, remember that while you hold onto that question, it will keep you confused and tormented. I don't know what you have gone through or what you have suffered, but I guess that there wouldn't be a good enough reason to explain the pain you have experienced.

I encourage you to come to the Lord in prayer and let it go. Set some time aside as soon as possible to bring your questions to God and tell Him that you choose to give up the right to know. Tell Him that you are leaving your questions behind you and putting your trust in Him instead. Giving up on “why” sets you free to trust God once again and to believe Him for your complete healing.

Prayer

Dear Lord,

I have decided today to give up my right to answers. I have chosen to stop asking why and instead I lay this at Your feet. I don’t need to know why anymore. I sacrifice the right to know. I give up my demands and I ask for Your perfect peace. Take away the chaos and confusion. Let Your peace fill my heart and surround my mind today.

I lean on you and I entrust my heart and my whole life into your care. Heal me, Lord.

In Jesus’ name,

Amen.

Chapter 13

The bottomless pit of insecurity

"I held him and would not let him go..." Song of Songs 3:4

One of the most common consequences of a traumatic life is insecurity. In fact, irrespective of upbringing, there are not many people in this world who are totally free from insecurity, but I would encourage you to become one of them!

After years of living with rejection or abuse, we can end up believing that we are not good enough. To help us feel more secure, we develop coping mechanisms. All too often these techniques for relieving our insecurity become habits. But if we are to live life to the full and function as healthy human beings our behaviour will have to change.

We see the deep insecurity of the Shulamite and how it made her react. Let's look again at the passage in chapter 3 of Song of Songs.

> ***"By night on my bed I sought the one I love; I sought him but I did not find him. 'I will rise now,' I said, 'And go about the city; in the streets and in the squares I will seek the one I love.' I sought him but did not find him. The watchmen who go about the city found me; I said, 'Have***

> ***you seen the one I love?' Scarcely had I passed by them, when I found the one I love. I held him and would not let him go until I brought him to the house of my mother..." Song of Songs 3:1-4***

The Shulamite overreacted to normal circumstances because of her own problems. Despite the extravagant love of her husband, she felt insecure in her relationship with him. A normal, healthy wife would not worry too much if her husband arrived home late, but the Shulamite was so insecure that only having him right beside her and clinging onto him for dear life was enough.

She could have sent out servants to look for him if she was concerned. However, insecurity is not rational. She got up late at night and went searching for him herself. The watchmen must have thought her behaviour very odd. Then when she found King Solomon, the Bible tells us that she would not let him go. Such needy behaviour can be exhausting for those around us.

I remember a habit of mine from our early years of marriage. Perhaps my husband had looked a little tired at bedtime or maybe I had been impatient earlier in the evening. It wouldn't be long before insecurity gripped me and filled my mind with rejection and fear. Just at the point when my husband was drifting off to sleep, I would blurt out, "Do you still love me?" or "Please can I have a hug?"

The first few times I did this, he responded with love and kindness. But soon it started to wear him down. Insecurity always makes demands on others. The Shulamite demanded that the King, despite the importance of his role, was at her side at all times because she needed his reassurance. Insecurity binds people whereas confidence releases them.

What's your fix?

Insecurity is compulsive. A feeling does not drive us to action. I can feel happy or sad, but I don't need to do anything about that feeling. However, when we are insecure, there is an irresistible craving for reassurance.

This may come from a hug, an acknowledgement or a smile. Perhaps a position in church makes you feel worthy or accepted. You may constantly prompt people for compliments, congratulations or words of affirmation. Or you may be someone who needs career success to reassure you that you are valuable and capable.

We all develop different strategies or 'habits' to satisfy our craving for reassurance. You know when you're starting to feel inadequate or insecure and so you prime someone to give you your 'shot' for the day. In your heart, you are crying out, "Affirm me, compliment me, respect me, recognise my gift." After someone has told you that you are brilliant, all is well until the craving builds again and you seek the drug of reassurance once more.

It can be dangerous

King Saul in the Old Testament was driven by insecurity and the desire to please people. There are countless examples of how the words and attitudes of the crowd influenced his decisions and therefore harmed his leadership. It's easy to think of Saul as 'the enemy', but remember that he was God's first choice as king over Israel. He loved the Lord and had the gift and call of leadership on his life. Nonetheless, in the end, regrettably his insecurities dominated his life.

When Saul conquered the enemies of Israel under the anointing of the Holy Spirit, the people praised his success. The King enjoyed the admiration of his subjects and fed off their approval. This is a very dangerous thing to do. I thank God for ministers who refuse to take any glory for the miracles that Jesus performs through them. It is God who gives gifts and it is God who deserves all the praise. We must never accept any credit for our gifting or success. We must always deflect any praise to heaven. If you do this in everything you carry out for the Lord, it will help keep you a safe distance from the approval of man.

Saul did not distance himself from people's applause and ended up deriving great satisfaction from man's approval. When it started to dry up and David attracted more attention, it ate away at him.

> ***"Saul has slain his thousands and David his ten thousands." 1 Samuel 18:7***

Saul was no longer getting his fix. He soon became obsessed with removing the 'obstacle' from his way and with eliminating the one who was stealing *his* approval. The people's remarks sowed the seeds of hatred in him. It led to a series of dreadful decisions and the desire to destroy a man after God's own heart. How serious insecurity becomes if we don't deal with it at the root.

Saul never learned to receive his adequacy and affirmation from God.

Instead, the hunger for approval grew and led to his final downfall. He crossed a religious boundary and contravened Judaic law by carrying out a ceremony that should only have been conducted by a priest. When Samuel arrived and saw what Saul had done, he was devastated and asked Saul for an explanation. Saul responded:

> ***"'When <u>I saw that people were scattered from me</u> and that you did not come... and that the Philistines gathered ... <u>I felt compelled</u>, and offered a burnt offering.' And Samuel said to Saul, 'You have done foolishly. You have not kept the commandment of the Lord your God which He commanded you. For now the Lord would have established your kingdom over Israel forever. But now your kingdom shall not continue.'" 1 Samuel 13:11-14***

Saul was driven by the need to please those around him. He did not act out of conviction or the desire to please God, but compulsion. Conviction enables us to make the right decisions; compulsion drives us to live our lives by the consent of others. In trying to please the people and protect his position, Saul displeased God and lost his position. If he had passed this test, history would have told a very different story: "For now the Lord would have established your kingdom over Israel forever. But now your kingdom shall not continue." (verse 14) Insecurity led to the downfall of a king chosen by God to lead His nation. Insecurity closed the door to his children and his children's children inheriting the throne.

Let's be honest

We do not need to depend on success, compliments, affection, affirmation, position, applause or anything else to feel secure. When our hearts are healed, we can draw on the assurance of God to meet our innermost needs. All other sources of confidence are like drugs, which satisfy for a moment and then leave us – the 'user' – feeling empty and in need of the next fix. The more an addict feeds a drug habit, the more he needs the drug and the more dependent he becomes.

So it is with us. If we feed insecurity with external reassurances, our dependency on those things will only grow. The truth is that when I look to man to make me feel secure, I am saying, "I am not enough without their approval. I am not sufficient without my latest success. I am not good enough without a job title or a position."

It used to make me feel important when I told people that I was the Director of Communications for a well-known organisation. How sad that I needed a good job title to make me feel significant. All the while, I was a daughter of my heavenly Father. Because I thought the world wouldn't value me without a title, I didn't value myself either. The Bible teaches us not to feed our insecurity with any position.

> ***"And do not be called teachers for One is your Teacher, the Christ." Matthew 23:10***

It's all too easy to find yourself doing the right things for the wrong reasons – in order to be noticed or thanked by leaders, teachers, bosses and others. We must learn to conquer insecurities.

> ***"But without your consent I wanted to do nothing, that your good deed might not be by compulsion, as it were, but voluntary." Philemon 14***

Christ is our All in All, the One who deserves every title of admiration and praise. He is also our example of perfect security. People spat at Him, hated Him, lied about Him, misunderstood Him, abandoned Him, betrayed Him, mocked Him, belittled Him and yet, through every trial and test, He remained secure. He knew *who* He was and *whose* He was.

Inadequate?

Have you ever felt intimidated by your surroundings or by the people around you? I used to get horribly edgy when I was with important or successful people. I would feel the need to prove that I was worthy and clever, but all too often I would fluff my opportunity to impress and feel terrible afterwards. By contrast, Jesus knew who He was and that His Father was with Him through thick and thin. He was able to say in His heart, "I am with My Father." (John 8:16)

When circumstances or people rock our stability, we can do as Jesus did. We can say, "I am with Him – my Daddy God." He is the One who formed us and chose us. He gives us legitimacy and the right to stand secure with our head held high, however superior the people around us may appear.

It is wonderful to be completely secure, at peace with who you are and safe in any circumstance. I believe that one of the most important revelations on perfect security can be found in Colossians. I suggest that you make this scripture your daily prayer and confession it until you believe it. Why don't you learn it by heart?

> ***"For in Him dwells all the fullness of the godhead in bodily form; and you are complete in Him..." Colossians 2:9-10***

You are complete in Him! Let me put it another way: in Jesus, you are enough - just the way you are. You are sufficient. You are accepted by God and any feelings of inadequacy will fall away as you receive a true realisation that you are whole in Him.

When your boss scowls at you or you don't get that promotion, confess, "I am complete in Christ." When you are undermined by colleagues or loved ones, remind yourself, "I am complete in Him. Jesus and I are enough. I don't need the acceptance or approval of anyone else."

It may take a while, but if you meditate on this word and ask the Holy Spirit to reveal its truth to your heart, you will be transformed by the renewing of your mind. You will learn to accept yourself, just the way you are.

Enjoy being you

Paul, by the Holy Spirit, put it another way in another letter, this time to the church at Corinth:

> ***"I am what I am by the favour of God..." 1 Corinthians 15:10***

Think on that and receive the peace and contentment that comes with it. The Lord knows you completely and loves you perfectly. You don't have to strive for acceptance or work for your adequacy. It is all yours in Christ Jesus.

Take time now to ask the Holy Spirit to show you any habits that you have depended on to allay your sense of insecurity. Come to Him in prayer and ask for His forgiveness for looking to anything or anyone other than Christ for reassurance. Then allow the words of Colossians 2 and 1 Corinthians 15 to fill your soul and invade your consciousness.

Next time you are compelled by insecurity to seek a compliment, some recognition or the respect of others, stop and turn to the Lord. Don't feed that habit anymore. Confess God's word over your life and let Him know that your security and adequacy comes from Him.

> ***"And it shall come to pass in that day that the remnant of Israel and those who have escaped will never again depend on him who defeated (struck) them, but will depend on the Lord, the Holy One of Israel in truth." Isaiah 10:20***

Don't be too hard on yourself

Statistics from Britain's National Health Service indicate that it takes the average smoker eighteen attempts to finally quit. The UK government once ran a poster campaign aimed at addicts with the strapline:

"DONT GIVE UP GIVING UP"

It is one of the most important messages you and I need to remember. Our healing process is a journey. The Bible says about those who trust in God:

> ***"A righteous man may fall seven times, yet he will arise again." Proverbs 24:16***

If you slip, don't be discouraged. Simply dust yourself off and receive God's wonderful love once again. Pick up your Bible verses, start to believe them and confess them over your life again. It may take a while, but you will get there in the end. It's worth waiting for. When you first realise how secure you have become, it will put the biggest smile on your face.

Prayer

Father God,

I don't want to lean on anyone or anything other than You for my security.

I am sorry that I have relied on (*name what has been giving you your 'fixes' – job titles, compliments, recognition etc*) and I ask You to forgive me. I choose to turn away from man and instead I look to You for my wholeness.

I thank You that I am complete in You. Through You, I am enough. In You, I am adequate.

I thank You that I am the way I am by Your favour. I am fearfully and wonderfully made. Wherever I go, You are right beside me.

From now on, I will look to You for my security and I will seek You for affirmation. You are all I need.

I am so grateful and I give You praise!

In Jesus' name,

Amen.

Chapter 14

The fear of history repeating itself

"The watchmen who went about the city found me. They struck me, they wounded me; the keepers of the walls took my veil away from me." Song of Songs 5:7

As the healing love of God starts to flow through your life, your inner image will be rebuilt and your heart cleansed. There will be a fresh sense of freedom and joy.

However, one problem that some face as they are becoming whole is the fear of history repeating itself. You are stronger and better, but as soon as you encounter even a whiff of hurtful behaviour, anxiety arises.

The Shulamite had suffered rejection and abuse as she was growing up. Now she was married to the King and therefore commanded the respect of the nation. However, as we saw in the last chapter, she was still terribly insecure and tormented by fears of violence and abuse.

Dreams are often a photograph of our inner thoughts and fears. When we refuse to think about something, our subconscious mind will push it to the surface through our dreams. If you have dreamt about negative experiences of the past, you need to ask God to show you why. Perhaps you are not healed or maybe you are still living under fear or shame.

The Shulamite had a bad dream. In chapter 5 of Song of Songs, she dreamt that the King came to her bedroom late at night. She didn't get up straight away because she was already undressed and in bed, but of course she wanted to be with him. By the time she arose and went to the door, he had gone:

> ***"I opened for my beloved, but my beloved had turned away and was gone. My heart leapt up when he spoke. I sought him, but I could not find him; I called him but he gave me no answer." Song of Songs 5:6***

The Shulamite was terrified of losing her husband. The rejection of the past had produced deep fears. She was afraid that she would blow it, that she would make a wrong move or a terrible mistake and her perfect life would come crashing down around her. But the dream didn't stop there. Compelled by the fear of rejection and insecurity, she got up in the middle of the night and went about searching for her husband the King.

When anxiety dictates our decisions, things normally get worse. As she searched the streets, she was attacked and abused by the watchmen - the very people who were supposed to be guarding the city, the King, the Queen and its citizens:

> ***"The watchmen who went about the city found me. They struck me, they wounded me; the keepers of the walls took my veil away from me." Song of Songs 5:7***

The Shulamite no longer suffered abuse, but it was still the fear of her heart. Her dreams exposed her unresolved anxieties.

I have ministered to many people who are gripped by the fear of rejection. They are afraid that the people they love most will abandon them or reject them. They are afraid that they will be 'found out' and their loved ones will discover that they aren't so lovable after all. After rejection, the fear of rejection can be one of the most debilitating difficulties to deal with. The beginning of our deliverance is to acknowledge that there is a problem.

Andy repeatedly rejected his wife. He was subconsciously convinced that she would follow the example of his mother and every other woman in his life and reject him. So he pushed her away at any time he thought she was going to hurt him. Inevitably, his deep-seated fear of being rejected by her wounded him as well as his true love. Thank God she stood by him until he was healed and restored.

Facing your fears

We must face our fears and break their power over our lives. The first step is accepting the truth and telling God, "I am afraid of being rejected again, of being hurt one more time." The Bible says there is no fear in love and that perfect love casts out fear. Admit the truth that you are afraid and ask God to fill your heart again with His love.

In the Psalms, David confessed the words, "I put my trust in you", more than forty times. Trusting God is a deliberate decision and it is in direct opposition to fear. Come to God in prayer and make a decision to put your trust in Him. Tell Him that you trust Him with your heart and your life. Tell Him that you know He is big enough and strong enough to take care of you. While fear controls your life, you will never be happy or free. When you overcome fear, I can tell you from personal experience that it is exhilarating!

> ***"For God has not given us a spirit of fear, but of power, love and of a sound mind." 2 Timothy 1:7***

Why do you think that God mentions power and a sound mind, alongside love, as enemies of fear? Fear paralyses us and it impairs sound thought and judgement. It's very difficult to behave rationally and lovingly when we are driven by fear. But you do not have to live under its control. Fear of rejection, fear of abandonment, fear of bereavement, fear of man – whatever form fear takes – it is always a trap:

> ***"The fear of man brings a snare, but he who trusts in the Lord shall be safe." Proverbs 29:25***

Fearing man for any reason is like a noose around your neck. Left unchallenged, fear will control you and mess up your thinking, your decisions and your behaviour. It wrecks relationships and robs its victims of peace and happiness.

In contrast, choosing to trust God makes you completely safe. The word 'safe' as it appears in Proverbs 29:25 actually means secure or set on high. Trusting God is the safest place to be. It's the place of perfect security, out of reach of the threats and taunts of the enemy.

You can take authority over the spirit of fear. Freedom from its grip is a huge relief that brings incredible joy. You don't have to tolerate fear any longer. God's Word in your mouth is as powerful as God's Word in His mouth. The Bible says, "Resist the devil and he *will* flee from you." (James 4:7)

Fear and faith are diametrically opposed. The Bible says, "Anything that is not of faith is sin." (Romans 14:23) So the way to start dealing with fear is by acknowledging that fear is sin. Go to God in prayer and tell Him that you are sorry for fearing. Renounce all fear from your life and then rebuke the spirit of fear.

Make a deliberate decision to trust God. We shouldn't trust people first, but God's ability to watch over us and take care of us. Anytime you sense fear trying to creep up again, rebuke it and again make a decision: "I put my trust in God." Be free from fear – it is not your portion.

Memories and flashbacks

Memories of the past can become objects of dread. They can be like rooms in the vast expanses of our mind that we dare not open because the contents are too painful. When something opens the door, we recoil as quickly as possible. We try to turn our faces away so that we don't have to witness the sight, feel the pain or experience the shame again. Often we think that by avoiding those recollections, we are helping ourselves to recover or preventing self-pity.

The problem is that if you avoid your memories, the enemy can use them to trip you up whenever he chooses. We can end up being just as afraid of those memories as we might have been of rejection. And as we know, fear is an enemy of God.

There are certain memories that used to hold me bound. I would try to turn away to stop myself from experiencing the pain of the past again.

When I woke up on the days immediately after our dear daughter died, I would sometimes forget the loss for a few moments. The thing that usually reminded me of her death was the empty space in the corner of our bedroom where her baby listening monitor used to sit. Somehow that sight had the power to send me into a spin.

I would first remember my little girl lying unwell on my tummy in the middle of the night. I would remember my fear and think about her sweet frame snuggling close to mine. Then I would soon find myself back in that horrible place of panic and despair, not knowing what to do. Soon, I would see her asleep in the morning as I went to work. I would watch myself leave the house. Next, I would be on the train travelling into London and I would hear that mobile phone call with my husband and the angst in our voices. Finally, I would receive that message. Naomi had been rushed to hospital in an ambulance and I must leave work immediately. I would see the corner of the hotel meeting room where I was standing as I listened to that fateful voicemail message. I got to the hospital as quickly as possible, but the rest is history. Once or twice the memories sucked me into deep dread so powerfully that I suffered from a panic attack.

There have been other memory cycles that have gripped me at different times of my life as well. They have all tended to be linked to shame or regret.

The way out

I once attended a Christian leadership conference and met a doctor who ran a training session about ministering to people who suffered from panic attacks. I remember silently weeping my way through the down-to-earth workshop and then asking for prayer at the end. I learned a very important lesson that day:

While we run away from painful memories, we stay bound by the fear and pain of those events. If you suffer from flashbacks, I want to encourage you to face the memories that have held you captive. Next time someone or something opens the door to that room or those rooms in your heart, don't run away.

Instead, invite the Holy Spirit to come in and ask Jesus to heal you of the pain of that memory. Look at the pictures of your past. Examine the memories that try to overwhelm you and tell the Lord how much they hurt. He is faithful and kind so when you ask Him in faith to heal your memories, He will answer.

After that session with the Christian doctor, I brought every painful memory to Jesus and made a decision that day to never run from the past again. I knelt down before the Lord in prayer and asked Him to heal my heart. I told Him I would never again be afraid of the past or its memories. I pledged to bring every picture to Him when they came to mind.

I was never again sucked into a downward spiral of flashbacks and I never again had a panic attack. I was not yet whole, but I was certainly getting healed. Instead of running away from my pain, I was bringing my pain to the only true Healer. Memories were no longer a source of dread and denial. They now became an opportunity to get a little bit more healed.

He will do for you what He did for me and what He has done for so many others. When you face the truth, you remove fear and anxiety and you can have faith in God's ability to restore you. One by one, He will remove the sting from your unwritten memoirs.

Old Ghosts

The people who hurt us most can become giants in our minds. There may be someone whose very name makes you shudder. When you see their number flash up on your phone, your stomach turns and you fall apart inside.

Perhaps you no longer see the person, but you frequently imagine how you would react if you bumped into them. The enemy will try to use the memory of that individual to torment you even when you are safe and secure.

There needs to come a time when you face these people in your heart and deal with the sting. Picture yourself coming before those who have hurt you the most. See yourself before them, no longer afraid or intimidated. Ask the Lord to fill your heart with godly love for that person or persons. Ask Him to show you how He sees them.

Often people have their own problems and insecurities and as a result you might never be able to hold a face-to-face talk with them about the past. Or perhaps they have passed away. Either way, you can have the conversation without them, but in the presence of God.

You may need to brace yourself, choosing to no longer react or recoil. Whatever was dysfunctional in your relationship with that person is what you need to deal with in prayer. Don't let the memory of anyone - living or dead - hold you to ransom. Jesus has set you free!

The Shulamite had to face her brothers once again. They made some provocative comments that would have crushed her at one time:

> ***"We have a little sister and she has no breasts. What shall we do for our little sister in the day when she is spoken for? If she is a wall, we will build upon her a battlement of silver" Song of Songs 8:8***

The Shulamite would probably have been quite happy if she had never seen her brothers again. However, the Spirit of Truth always guides us into restoration, and in some instances that means confrontation. Here she faces once again the patronising taunts of her brothers. They seem intent on bringing the shadows of the past into her new life with the King. I wouldn't be surprised if they were jealous. They may also have been afraid. Perhaps the way they treated their little sister would come back to haunt them now that she was such a powerful woman.

But just like Joseph, the Shulamite refused to return evil for evil. We see how the healing love of the King gave her the assurance to face the past. With a new garment of acceptance and honour wrapped around her, she lovingly confronted their comments.

> ***"I am a wall and my breasts are like towers;" Song of Songs 8:10***

She was saying, "Everything has changed. I am strong now and I am independent of you. You can't hurt me any longer, nor can you build your lives on me. I am not your property. I belong to the King." I love the following words in scripture. This lady reached a place of contentment and peace. She closes this verse by saying:

> ***"Then I became in his eyes as one who found peace." Song of Songs 8:10b***

After a lifetime of pain and following a healing process in the arms of the King, our heroine found peace. Peace is available to you as you allow God to deal with the past.

Prayer

Father God,

I realise that I have lived in the shadow of fear. I have been intimidated by the thoughts of history repeating itself in my life. But I don't want to live under the control of fear for another day.

I repent for allowing fear into my life. I am sorry that I have submitted to intimidation and allowed it to control and torment me. I know that fear is sin so I ask you to cleanse me from all unrighteousness.

Now I take my stand. In Jesus' name, I rebuke the spirit of fear. I drive you out of my life and break your power over me. I have not been given the spirit of fear, but of power, love and a sound mind. Holy Spirit, come in your power and fill me afresh.

Where memories have had power over me, I now face those pictures and ask You to heal me of their pain. I will not run away from glimpses of past events and anytime I remember a painful experience, I will ask You to heal me.

Where negative thoughts about a person (or persons) have gripped me, I bring that individual to You. I see myself meeting them and I choose to be assertive, but polite. (Name of person) I am not afraid of you anymore. Once I was hurt, but now I'm being healed. Once I was weak, but now I am becoming strong. Only Jesus has control of my life now.

Father, I thank You that You are making me whole. Nothing and no one can hold me anymore and I give You praise!

In Jesus' name, I pray,

Amen.

Chapter 15

Wanted!

"I am my beloved's, and his desire is towards me." Song of Songs 7:10

One of the consequences of rejection is the sense that you don't really belong. If those who are supposed to love us neglect their responsibilities or push us away, we can end up feeling abandoned. In order to protect ourselves, we become detached from the people around us. Sometimes we build walls to keep them out. That way we think we are safe. We can live in the midst of a loving congregation or circle of friends, yet feel alone. My husband calls it the spirit of abandonment.

The Bible says that God puts the solitary (those who are alone) in families (Psalm 68:6). He says that we are to be one, just as He is one with the Son and the Spirit (John 17:21). To enjoy life to the full, we need to leave isolation behind. As we open up and share the secrets of our hearts with those closest to us, the walls start to come down. But the real transformation happens when we exchange our feelings of abandonment for the truth that we belong.

In the Song of Songs, marriage represents the end of one era and the beginning of another. For the Shulamite, abandonment and rejection had finished and a new day of love and acceptance had dawned.

You may have been rejected in the past, but Jesus has chosen you and has taken you as His own. Once, you may have been despised, but now you are dearly loved. Once, perhaps, you were driven away, but now you have been brought near.

The Shulamite was no longer alone because she now belonged to the King. We know that her brothers still lurked in the shadows and that she still grappled with some old fears. However, the truth was that she belonged.

Your worth is not determined by the people around you. Your value is settled by the King of Kings. You need to know that because the God of all creation treasures you, you are priceless.

The Shulamite regularly and proudly declared, "I am my beloved's and he is mine." In knowing that she belonged to the King, this young woman found self-worth and security. Let's look at Song of Songs 7:10 in several Bible translations. As you read, allow the words to penetrate your soul - this is the Father's heart towards you.

> ***"I am my lover's and he claims me as his own." New Living Translation***
>
> ***"I am my lover's. I'm all he wants. I'm all the world to him!" The Message***
>
> ***"[She proudly said] I am my beloved's, and his desire is toward me!" Amplified***

Allow these phrases to sink in: the King of Kings claims you as His own; you mean the world to your heavenly Father; He wants you to be with Him and to be known as His; you belong.

I have watched men and women who have grown up in single parent or loveless families crave the approval of a mum or a dad. They are drawn to mother and father figures who they hope will nurture them. There is almost a magnetic pull towards parental personalities. And being affirmed and encouraged by such people instils a measure of self-worth and stability. However, until we know and accept the love and kindness of God, no human love will satisfy us. Until we receive the Lord God as our Father, no earthly love will be enough.

You need to know that Jesus has taken you to be His own. Through Jesus, God the Father adopts you as His son or daughter. You are family, you are loved and you are His - no matter what. You are not abandoned, you belong.

I want the world to know

The Shulamite regularly reminded herself that the King had taken her to be his own and that he loved her dearly. I'm sure stability and assurance grew in her heart every time she spoke the words, "I am my beloved's and he is mine!" When we declare biblical truth over our lives in faith, we seal it in our hearts. Our tongue directs the course of our life (James 3:3-4), so as we speak His Word, we will soon start to believe it in our hearts.

Put God's words of love and acceptance in your mouth today by faith. Confess that you belong, that you are loved, that you are valuable. Don't just reflect on Bible verses, speak them over your life. That releases faith and power. Join the Shulamite and make a new declaration over your life today: "I belong to Jesus. He claimed me as His own because He wants me. I belong and I am wanted. I have a Father who will never, ever fail me and I have a Brother who will never leave me or let me down."

King Solomon understood the power of his words over his wife's life. I thank God for the generation I'm part of and the teaching of the last twenty or thirty years. My husband and I have watched the words that we have spoken over our children since the day they were born. We work hard to make sure that we don't utter negative or controlling statements about them or to them.

When they are badly behaved, we tell them that their behaviour is naughty - not that *they* are naughty. We tell them constantly that they are loved, wonderful, clever, chosen children. Neither our son nor our daughter has issues with self-confidence or self-esteem and I am so grateful to God for this.

But that is not the pattern in many households. If you grew up without words of affirmation, you need to fill the void with God's wonderful Word. As a teenager, I confessed God's words of love and approval over my life. I identified the scriptures that spoke of God's acceptance of me and I would confess them over and over again.

> ***"Oh what manner of love the Father has lavished upon us that we should be called children of God. And that is what we are!" 1 John 3:1***

> ***"I will praise you, for I am fearfully and wonderfully made; marvellous are your works and that my soul knows very well." Psalm 139:14***

Personalise scriptures like these by saying, "Oh what manner of love the Father has lavished on me that I should be called a child of God. And that is who I am!" Believe and speak God's Word that you were wonderfully made and that you are a marvellous creation. Eventually your soul will come to know the truth.

The King declared his unchanging love over the Shulamite so often that she had the confidence to tell the world about it. Think about that for a moment. Not many people talk freely about how much they are loved, especially those from a dysfunctional family. Yet the Shulamite had the confidence to proclaim her husband's love for her:

> ***"He brought me to His banqueting house and his banner over me is love." Song of Songs 2:4b***

This demonstrates the scale of God's love and acceptance. He places a signpost over your head that says, "Wanted!" He wants the world to know that you are His and that He loves you. The banner over your life is no longer "rejected", "unwanted" or "not good enough". The banner now is love.

Prayer

Heavenly Father,

I thank You that You chose me because You love me and I thank you that I belong to You. You are my Father and You have adopted me as Your own. I accept and embrace my adoption. I am now Yours and You are mine! It's not a temporary commitment which You have made to me. It's for life. We belong together and You will never leave me or let me down.

I praise You, I love You and I thank You for making me Your own.

In Jesus' name, I pray,

Amen.

Chapter 16

A new beginning

"Rise up, my love, my fair one and come away. For lo, the winter is past..." Song of Songs 2:10-11

God is the God of new beginnings. Some time ago, I was in hospital with my daughter, Abigail, who needed a major operation. We spent about two weeks on a neurosurgical ward at Great Ormond Street Hospital for Children. During that time, I got to know some of the staff pretty well. Just before we left, I talked to a nurse who was flicking through Abigail's medical notes. She came upon an entry at the front of the file which said we had lost our first child. She was shocked that she hadn't already detected that we were a family who had suffered such a tragedy.

After decades in nursing, she prided herself on her ability to spot traumatised people. In her opinion, losing one child and then watching another deal with a serious illness was more than enough to break the average family into pieces. What she didn't know was that when God heals, He does it perfectly and completely. It's as if you never suffered in the first place. We weren't living under the shadow of tragedy. We had been made whole again and we were given a new beginning. That nurse was touched by the love and healing power of God as I shared our testimony.

When I look back on my life, I am filled with gratitude. Restoration changed my perspective and I can now see the goodness of God in the midst of the storm. I recognise His hand of protection and kindness. I appreciate people who I once regarded as sources of pain. You will know you are becoming whole when you can look back at your life and experience genuine joy and thanks for what God has done.

As you start to come through a season of healing, God in His wonderful mercy will begin to draw a line under the past. I believe that we are always work in progress. We will never 'arrive', but we can reach a place of health and wholeness; a place of rest and peace. In this world, tribulation is guaranteed and things will happen that hurt us. We need to learn to seek and receive healing as we go. However, there will come a time when the majority of your healing is complete. This is a time for rejoicing and celebrating. It's like a change of season. Winter comes to an end and spring arrives. It's time to arise and to strengthen yourself in the Word of God.

> ***"Rise up, my love, my fair one and come away. For lo, the winter is past, the rain is over and gone. The flowers appear on the earth; the time of singing has come, and the voice of the turtledove is heard in our land... Rise up my love, my fair one and come away!" Song of Songs 2:10-13***

As your healing season comes to an end, allow the praises of God to rise from your heart more and more. Meditate on God's promises of your new beginning and make them your own. Believe and confess God's Word concerning your new life and destiny. Healing is important, but it is only one part of God's plan for you. Abundant life is the goal!

There is a time for choosing to move on. This is not because you are denying anything, but because you are ready to live life to the full.

> ***"Do not remember the former things, nor consider the things of old. Behold, I do a new thing, now it shall spring forth; shall you not know it?" Isaiah 43:18***

The time to move on is as important as the time to face the truth. It's an opportunity to put your hope and trust in Him and to look forward to the great blessings that God has in store for you:

> ***"Behold the former things have come to pass and new things I declare." Isaiah 42:9***

> ***"I will make a road in the wilderness and rivers in the desert. The beast of the field will honour Me, the jackals and the ostriches, because I give waters in the wilderness and rivers in the desert, to give drink to My people, My chosen." Isaiah 43:18-20***

Prayer

Father God,

Thank You for Your awesome healing work in my life. I am overwhelmed by Your love and Your goodness. The past is behind me and all things have become new. I am a new creation and I have a fresh start. I thank You that the plans You have for me are plans to prosper me and not to harm me, to give me a hope and a bright future.

I look ahead now to all Your promises. I thank You that You will use me in wonderful ways to bring Your love and kindness into the lives of others.

I love You, I thank You for everything You have done and I praise You for what lies ahead.

In Jesus' name,

Amen.

Chapter 17

Restoration

"I will restore to you the years the locust has eaten..." Joel 2:25

There is a difference between healing and restoration. Let me explain. Imagine a contract worker who is paid only for the time he spends at the office. Let's say this worker breaks his leg and spends four weeks off work. God might miraculously heal his leg and enable him to get back to the office. But if God restored this man, he would be healed AND all the losses returned to him for the time he was out of work. God is a God of healing and restoration.

I got saved as a teenager and I loved the Lord with all of my heart. However, when I went to university, I sought love and reassurance in all the wrong places. I eventually backslid. I drank too much and got into a very unhealthy relationship. I was already damaged by a difficult family life and this five-year period of waywardness nearly finished me off. I remember the day I rededicated my life to the Lord as if it was yesterday...

I was walking through a park in central London thinking about the state of my life. I remembered a song I used to sing: "In my life, Lord, be glorified, be glorified..." I mused on those words, considering it virtually impossible for God to be glorified through my messed-up life. Then I heard a quiet voice in my heart sing the last line of that song: "In my life, Lord, be glorified *today*."

I was struck by the word *'today'*. I thought to myself, "I have no idea how anything good could come from my future, but I have enough faith to believe that God could do something good with me today." I made a monumental decision. I left a place of loneliness and alienation from God to surrender my broken life to Him once again.

That was the beginning of the rest of my life, but I had lost five long years. One of the issues that troubled me as I turned my life back to the Lord was that I should have known better. I had come to Jesus as a teenager and yet I walked away from Him in my twenties. Then God spoke to me. He gave me a promise:

> ***"So I will restore to you the years that the swarming locust has eaten, the crawling locust, the consuming locust, and the chewing locust... You shall eat in plenty and be satisfied and praise the name of the Lord your God who has dealt wondrously with you." Joel 2:25-26***

It was only a matter of months before my life was back on track. God provided a new home for me and two wonderful female flatmates. He found me a new church where I was built up and empowered. He also gave me a new ministry leading a small team of street evangelists. My prayer life was back on track and my nose was in the Word. After messing up and missing out, God put me right back in the centre of His will. I had a lot to learn, but

I was back where I belonged. Our God is faithful and His plan is to restore. Eventually, it will be as though you were never damaged in the first place.

> ***"I have loved you with an everlasting love; therefore with loving-kindness I have drawn you. Again I will build you and you shall be rebuilt... and you shall go forth in the dances of those who rejoice." Jeremiah 31:3-4***

God's type of restoration is total restoration. He won't just heal you. He will rebuild your life until it's happier and more blessed than it would have been if you had not suffered.

> ***"I will turn their mourning to joy, I will comfort them and make them rejoice rather than sorrow...I will fill to the full the soul of the priests with abundance and My people shall be satisfied (filled abundantly) with My goodness, says the Lord." Jeremiah 31:13-14***

It's time to believe God for the very best. Not just for yourself, but for those you love as well. God will turn your life around to such an extent that the very issues that were sources of pain now become sources of joy as He uses you to help people who have suffered in similar ways. As they are healed, you will be filled with gladness.

I am forever grateful to God for the many occasions that He has used me to bring hope and healing to bereaved people. I know that I will be reunited with Naomi again in heaven, and while I'm still here, God uses me to bring comfort to those who are grieving. It's an incredible privilege.

Even the mistakes I made bring me joy now. I can look back and see the power of the blood of Jesus to eradicate all sin and to give double honour to those who have messed up. When people learn of my backslidden years, it gives them hope that their own lives can be turned around. Everything that the enemy meant for my harm, God has turned around for my good and the good of others. That's restoration!

I have watched countless people be healed and then also go on to see their lives fully restored. Tony came from a lineage of male-dominated marriages where unhealed, insecure fathers ruled their families with an iron rod. Tony and his wife Vera now run a marvellous marriage ministry and bring help and wisdom to countless couples. Through their healing, entire families have been set free.

A friend who was abused when she was growing up now ministers to those who have suffered similar violation. God uses her to bring hope and recovery. My husband, who was raised in abject poverty, now brings the message of prosperity to the poor. Now that's what I call restoration.

As you consider your life, I encourage you to believe God for a total turnaround in every area. Ask Him to reverse your captivity, just like God did for Job in the Bible. Whatever has been hurt or damaged, ask God to bring life and hope to you and through you.

If you were abandoned, God could use you to bring healing to those who have suffered in similar ways. If you were out of work or ministry due to the circumstances of your life, ask God to restore the years you lost. Believe that He will bring you to the place where you would have been if you had never had 'time out'.

God delights in turning the tables. He delights in showing the enemy that he has lost. He delights in bringing real joy and happiness to a life that was once broken.

What do you desire? God is able!

Prayer

Father God,

You are faithful! You are my Healer and my Restorer. I thank You that the devil will regret the day he attacked my life. I pray for complete restoration, that You would use the areas of my life that were damaged to bring me and others genuine joy. I thank You that You are delighted when we rise up whole.

I give my entire life to You and ask You to use me for Your glory. I am excited about what You will do.

I give You all the glory and all the thanks.

In Jesus' name,

Amen.

In closing

Healing is a journey. The most important thing is that you are on the way. Your experiences and your healing process will be unique. Don't worry if you haven't yet reached your destination, because if you keep your eyes on Jesus, I know you will get there in the end. Just like the Shulamite, you will reach a point when you say, "Then I became in His eyes as one who found peace."

Would you like to invite Jesus into your heart?

If you would like to ask Jesus to become the Lord of your life, I would be honoured to lead you in a simple prayer. The Bible says that God loves you and that Jesus wants to draw close:

> ***"Behold I stand at the door and knock. If anyone hears My voice and opens the door, I will come in." Revelation 3:20***

If you would like to know Jesus as your friend, Lord and Saviour, the first step is asking. Pray this prayer:

Dear Lord

I know that You love me and have a good plan for my life. I ask You to come into my heart today and be my Lord. I give my life to You and ask You to lead me in Your ways from now on.

In Jesus' name,

Amen

About the author

Together with her husband Paul, Jo Naughton pastors Harvest Church in London, England. Jo is used by God across Europe and Africa to minister healing and restoration and to bring truth and clarity to men and women about everyday issues. Paul and Jo have two children, Benjamin and Abigail.

Lightning Source UK Ltd.
Milton Keynes UK
UKOW04f2202251017
311645UK00001B/34/P

9 781908 596673